By Cindy De La Hoz

Marilyn monroe

Platinum **FOX**

By Cindy De La Hoz

Marilyn monroe

Platinum FOX

By Cindy De La Hoz

RUNNING PRESS

PHILADELPHIA · LONDON

To Trisha

9 8 7 6 5 4 3 2
Digit on the right indicates the number of this printing

Library of Congress Control Number: 2007920074

ISBN-13: 978-0-7624-3133-5

Designed by Joshua McDonnell
Typography: Caslon, Century Gothic, and Cocktail

This book may be ordered by mail from the publisher.
Please include $2.50 for postage and handling.
But try your bookstore first!

Running Press Book Publishers
2300 Chestnut Street
Philadelphia, PA 19103-4371

Visit us on the web!
www.runningpress.com

Table of Contents

It was the 1950s. 20th Century-Fox saw the evolution of the platinum legend who still captivates at first sight. Marilyn's magnetism, her rare combination of sexiness and vulnerability, and specialized voice and bearing met with the artists and technicians of Fox in the creation of the ultimate star. The difficulties of her personal life are well-documented. Hours of waiting for an anxious Marilyn to arrive on the set could be followed by a dozen takes or more, but the magic between her and the camera always prevailed, and the effect on the screen was galvanizing. It all came together at Fox, where her twenty films for the studio grossed over two hundred million dollars, making her at the time, one of the top box-office stars Hollywood had ever known.

Over the years, Fox cultivated the careers of Will Rogers, Shirley Temple, Tyrone Power, Henry Fonda, Betty Grable, and many other stars, but with the passage of time, Marilyn became the jewel of the studio's crown. In July of 1946, a model named Norma Jeane made her first screen test on the set of the latest Betty Grable musical. It was the beginning of a union marked by tumultuous ups, downs, and trial separations. Still, the relationship extended over the fifteen-year length of her career as an actress and produced some of the best-loved films of the '50s.

Once her stardom was established, Marilyn and studio head Darryl Zanuck were frequently at odds over the direction of her career. Able to play the "dumb blonde" roles she was frequently given better than anyone, she was not against appearing in comedies, but there came a time when she wanted to be taken more seriously for her acting abilities. To achieve this, she was not only willing but determined to improve. Just when her career was at its zenith, Marilyn left Hollywood, only to return to Fox after she had taken lessons from some of the foremost acting instructors in the profession.

Marilyn's career at Fox makes a fascinating look at a star's development in the studio era. In her twenty Fox films she worked with some of the all-time great writers and directors (Billy Wilder, Howard Hawks, Otto Preminger, Joshua Logan, George Cukor, Joseph L. Mankiewicz—the list goes on). These collaborations at one of the best filmmaking facilities in Hollywood brought about moments that are at turns among the most humorous, stunning, joyous, poignant, and unforgettable ever filmed.

Perhaps the most positive way to explore the star in keeping with the spirit of Marilyn at her best is by her image on the screen. She is the perfect subject for a book focused on films because her technique was distinctly cinematic. A camera close up captured her subtle style in a face that registered the full range of emotions called upon to bring a character to life. The films are eternal testaments of Marilyn's talent and beauty. They keep her immortal.

QUINTESSENTIAL MARILYN AT FOX IN 1953

Act One: Beginnings

"I don't care about money. I just want to be wonderful."
—MARILYN

Norma Jeane Mortensen, the girl born and raised near the film capital of Hollywood in a series of homes with foster families and only briefly with her mother, sat in movie theaters at every available opportunity, enthralled by the magic before her. She needed little encouragement from David Conover, the photographer who found her working in an aircraft factory, to enter the world of show business. As a beautiful eighteen-year-old, Norma Jeane took her first modeling jobs, which quickly led to dozens of magazine covers.

In July 1946, at the age of twenty, she turned up at the office of 20th Century-Fox casting director Ben Lyon, whom she so impressed that he arranged for a color screen test of her, to be made under the best possible conditions with some of the studio's top crew members. The reaction to the test from production chief Darryl Zanuck was positive. As a result, Norma Jeane was signed to a $75 per week contract, and her name was soon changed to Marilyn Monroe. "Marilyn" was Lyon's suggestion, after stage performer Marilyn Miller, and the surname belonged to Norma Jeane's grandmother, Della Monroe.

During the six months that followed, the newly christened Marilyn posed for publicity photos, took acting lessons, and observed; a great advantage of being a studio contract player was that she could go to different departments and study any aspect of the cinema process in which she took an interest. One thing Marilyn did not do during this period was appear in any films, but still her contract was renewed on February 10, 1947. After that she was assigned just two bit parts and may have worked as an extra in other films, including *The Shocking Miss Pilgrim* and *Green Grass of Wyoming*, although these credits are not confirmed by studio records. When Marilyn's contract came up for renewal again, in August 1947, the decision was to let her go.

MARILYN

NOT YET THE BLONDE BOMBSHELL, STILL A BEAUTIFUL GIRL-NEXT-DOOR TYPE IN THE LATE '40S.

"Hi Rad!"

—Memorable only as the enthusiastic first words uttered by Marilyn Monroe on the screen. In color, wearing a blue pinafore, she can be identified only by freezing the frame as she greets the star of *Scudda Hoo! Scudda Hay!*, June Haver, while exiting a church. A distracted Haver, as farmgirl Rad McGill, half-heartedly replies, "Hi Betty."

Scudda Hoo! Scudda Hay! was based on a best-selling novel by George Agnew Chamberlain, which first appeared in installments in the magazine *Country Gentleman*. F. Hugh Herbert directed the film in addition to adapting the novel for the screen. For a time during post-production stages, the producers considered officially changing the title to *Summer Lightning* because they knew many moviegoers would not know the meaning of Chamberlain's original title. It is, in fact, a reference to commands occasionally called out by farmers to their mules when working. In the U.K., the film played in theaters as *Summer Lightning*.

MARILYN LOOKS AT PHOTOGRAPHS WITH LEADING CAST MEMBERS ROBERT KARNES AND LON MCCALLISTER
BETWEEN TAKES OF THE LAKESIDE SWIMMING AND ROWING SCENES.

One Man's Best Friends

Snug Dominy (Lon McCallister) is all but driven off of the Dominy family farm after his father leaves, himself in flight from Snug's cruel stepmother (Anne Revere) and her equally vicious son, Stretch (Robert Karnes). Snug goes to work for another ill-tempered character, Roarer McGill (Tom Tully), to whom he becomes indebted for the purchase of two mules which Snug arranges to pay off on an installment plan. Crowder and Moonbeam are a pair of stubborn mules who "drive" only for a chosen few. Under the guidance of his friend Tony (Walter Brennan), in order to land a job hauling lumber Snug learns quickly how to handle the mules, with the calls "scudda hoo, scudda hay."

Roarer's spirited daughter, Rad, likes Snug best of all her beaux, but resents his apparent preference for the company of mules and makes him jealous by flirting with Stretch. Snug has more worries after Roarer learns that the mules he sold to Snug can drive. Roarer schemes with Stretch to get them back. When Snug misses a payment on the mules, Roarer immediately calls in the sheriff, but Mrs. McGill (Geraldine Wall), knowing her husband is in the wrong, loans Snug the overdue funds.

Stretch, after a failed attempt at crippling the mules, is put off the Dominy land, along with his wicked mother. Rad could not be happier as the farm will be home to the future Mr. and Mrs. Snug Dominy. Crowder and Moonbeam come to the rescue when Roarer's tractor gets stuck in the mud. Snug thereby pays off his debt and wins the blessing of ornery old man McGill to marry Rad.

MARILYN AT THE CAST PARTY FOR *Scudda Hoo! Scudda Hay!*

WITH ROBERT KARNES AND LON MCCALLISTER

EYE-CATCHING MARILYN, SEATED BEHIND JUNE HAVER, IN A GROUP SHOT OF CAST
AND CREW MEMBERS OF HER FIRST FILM.

Snipped!

Marilyn experienced the occupational hazard of landing on the cutting room floor early on. In the spring of 1947, several months into her contract with Fox, *Scudda Hoo! Scudda Hay!* was the first film in which she was given a role. Insignificant, yes, but it was a start. Unfortunately, it almost vanished entirely. In addition to her momentary greeting to leading lady June Haver, Marilyn filmed another scene rowing on a lake, rating her billing as "Girl in a Canoe." The long shots on the lake that remain do not provide a close or clear enough view to confirm whether or not a glimpse of her scene at the lake made the final cut.

WHETHER OR NOT HER SCENES ON THE LAKE MADE THE FINAL PRINT, AT LEAST THESE PHOTOGRAPHS SHOW THAT MARILYN DID ENJOY HERSELF WITH HER FELLOW ACTORS AND CREW MEMBERS DURING REHEARSALS AND FILMING.

...At First Sight

Marilyn's work in *Scudda Hoo! Scudda Hay!* came first, but it was as Evie in *Dangerous Years* that moviegoers got their first true look at Marilyn Monroe. In production for just two weeks in July 1947, this low-budget film was directed by Arthur Pierson, who later led Marilyn through a slightly more significant role in a film which he also wrote and produced at MGM in 1951, *Hometown Story*.

"The Dangerous Years of Adolescence"

Danny Jones (Billy Halop), a newcomer in Middleton, is a corruptive influence on the city's youth, who now idle their time away at a roadhouse called the Gopher Hole in favor of the boys' club run by Jeff Carter (Donald Curtis). Danny leads several of the teenagers in the robbery of a warehouse. Jeff gets wind of the plot and tries to stop them. In his encounter with Danny, a gunshot is fired and Jeff is killed. The police round up the boys and Danny is put on trial for his life against a dogged District Attorney, Edgar Burns (Richard Gaines).

As the hard-fought case nears its close, Burns's daughter, Connie (Anabel Shaw), reveals a stunning truth as she fondly remembers Danny as the best friend of her childhood years spent in an orphanage. As a child, Connie was thought to be an orphan because her mother left Burns shortly after their marriage, concealing the fact that a baby was on the way. Many years passed before the orphanage matron, Miss Templeton (Nana Bryant), let Burns know of his child's existence.

Although Danny has a strong ally in Connie, her support does not alter the trial verdict—guilty. Miss Templeton arrives on the scene with startling news for Danny. The matron had let it be known that Connie was Burns's child in order to ensure medical treatment for the sickly girl. In reality, Burns is the father of Danny. Not wanting Connie to be hurt, Danny prevents the truth from becoming known, confesses that he is indeed guilty of killing Jeff Carter, and bravely accepts his sentence of life imprisonment.

Evie

One of the troublemaking youths, Gene, played by Dickie Moore, at least shows taste in his choice of girls. He has an eye for Evie, the Gopher Hole's prettiest waitress, who prefers Danny to Gene. Marilyn is shown in a number of medium close shots.

Evie's Exchanges

Gene: *"Hi Evie!"*
Evie: *"Hi Small Change."*
Gene: *"Hey wait. I got money tonight. Am I gonna see ya later?"*
Evie: *"If I'm not too tired."*
Gene: *"But Evie, I thought we had a date."*
Evie: *"Look, this tray weighs a ton."*

Gene: *"Miss — Two double cokes."*
Evie: *"Who's paying?"*
Gene: *"I told ya, I got money."*
Evie: *"And now you're blowing it on two cokes."*
Gene: *"Double!"*
Evie: *"My my!"*

Let Go . . .

By the time *Dangerous Years* was being shown in theaters, Fox had failed to renew Marilyn's contract and she was out. She signed on with Columbia in March 1948 and landed her first leading role, in *Ladies of the Chorus*, only to be dropped by Columbia when her contract came up for renewal six months after signing. She then appeared in the Mary Pickford-Lester Cowan-produced Marx Brothers film *Love Happy* before returning to the Fox lot once more.

··· A Ticket up North ·

A Ticket to Tomahawk took Marilyn on location to Durango in southwest Colorado, where she remained with a cast headed by two future co-stars, Dan Dailey and Anne Baxter, for five weeks in August and September 1949. Husband and wife writing partners Richard Sale and Mary Loos wrote the screenplay, for which Fox paid them $30,000. They later wrote the film version of *Gentlemen Marry Brunettes*, based of course on Mary's aunt Anita Loos's own sequel to her novel *Gentlemen Prefer Blondes*. Sale and Loos's work on *A Ticket to Tomahawk* was nominated for a Writers Guild Award.

The action of the story revolved around a railroad line that would later be designated as a National Historical Landmark. Fox had an agreement with the Rio Grande and Western Railroad for their Durango to Silverton line to serve as the setting for their train. The city of Denver, Colorado hosted the premiere of *A Ticket to Tomahawk* on April 18, 1950. The film also played in at least two cities as *The Sheriff's Daughter*. (The exhibitors did not mind that the girl in the story is the granddaughter of a marshal.)

MARILYN AND HER FELLOW SHOWGIRLS WITH THEIR MANAGER, PLAYED BY CONNIE GILCHRIST (LEFT).

THE WARDROBE WOMEN APPLY FINAL TOUCHES TO MARILYN'S COSTUME.

MARILYN FLOUTS DANGER WHILE ADJUSTING HER FISHNET HOSIERY.

IN THE END, THE LEAD CHARACTERS (JOHNNY AND KIT) NAME THEIR DAUGHTERS AFTER THE REAL NAMES OF THE ACTRESSES WHO PLAYED THE SHOWGIRLS: BARBARA, MARILYN, JOYCE, AND MARION.

"OH, WHAT A FORWARD YOUNG MAN YOU ARE," PERFORMED BY MARILYN AND THE GIRLS WITH DAN DAILEY.

MARION MARSHALL, BARBARA SMITH, JOYCE MACKENZIE, AND MARILYN SING BACK-UP FOR THE STAR.

THE GIRLS CAMP OUT OVERNIGHT. WHEN TOMBOY KIT, PLAYED BY ANNE BAXTER, ENTERS THEIR TENT, SHE IS STARTLED BY THEIR OVERNIGHT BEAUTY TREATMENTS.

A Train Trip

It is 1876 and the Tomahawk and Western's narrow gauge railway is making its inaugural run. To fulfill a franchise contract and ensure its future, the train must reach Tomahawk, Colorado on schedule, carrying at least one paying passenger. The trouble is, no one wants to travel by rail because a team of criminals, hired by the stagecoach line, are out to destroy the Tomahawk and Western.

The train is almost wrecked near the town of Epitaph. U.S. Marshal Dodge (Will Wright) assigns the duty of escorting the train safely to Tomahawk to his rough-and-ready granddaughter, Kit (Anne Baxter). Traveling man Johnny "Behind-the-Deuces" Jameson (Dan Dailey) is roped in to serve as the sole passenger, just as a gunman called Dakota (Rory Calhoun) joins the train troupe with the aim of sabotaging them before reaching Tomahawk.

To Dakota, his band of cutthroats, and a tribe of warring Indians, anything goes if it will keep the train from fulfilling its contract—even if it risks the lives of a quartet of young chorus girls. In spite of such formidable opposition, by journeys end the Indians have been converted to fight for the railway, the bad guys are toppled, the train reaches Tomahawk successfully, and Johnny and Kit have fallen in love.

True Troupers

Along its adventure, the history-making Tomahawk and Western is graced by the presence of "Madame Adelaide and her Sextet." The group consists of manager Madame Adelaide (Connie Gilchrist), her assistant, and four showgirls, the most beautiful of which is golden girl Clara (Marilyn), who wears yellow period costumes designed by Rene Hubert to match her blonde locks throughout.

Traveling to Tomahawk to fulfill an engagement, the troupe brightens a perilous trip with a song, "Oh, What a Forward Young Man You Are," in which they are joined by Dan Dailey. The girls are also game to help fight off Indians and clean and polish the train for its entry into Tomahawk.

∙ ∙ ∙ A Favorite Dress

Marilyn's wardrobe for her first scene in The Fireball, in which she is a spectator at the roller derby, came from her own closet. She appeared in the same sweater-dress on the screen a total of four times throughout 1950. It would get its widest exposure the next time she wore it, which was in the most acclaimed film of the year, *All About Eve*. The dress then reemerged on Marilyn in the film *Hometown Story*, and then finally in a screen test she made with Richard Conte in December 1950.

The scene in which Marilyn wears this dress is only one among many appearances she makes in the picture, each in a different set of clothes. She plays a rather snooty socialite-follower of the sport of competitive roller skating who shows up at all the events on the arm of her boyfriend (James Brown). The couple befriends Johnny Casar, played by Mickey Rooney, only because he is a skating star. Privately they dislike him, but that does not stop them from inviting him to their parties, where their friends join them in laughing at him. Fortunately for him, Eddie has such an inflated ego that he does not notice.

Speedway Drama

The plot of *The Fireball* (also known as *The Challenge*) was very loosely based on the life of Eddie Poore, a skating star of the Roller Speedway who was known professionally as Eddie Cazar. It was an independent production from Bert Friedlob, directed by Tay Garnett, and released by Fox.

After running away from an orphanage, Johnny Casar (Mickey Rooney) has no aim in life, except for a pair of skates that he comes upon by chance, which direct him to the local rink. Meeting professional skater Mary Reeves (Beverly Tyler) leads him to begin training to compete in the roller derby. Johnny first makes a name for himself by heckling skating star Mack Miller (Glenn Corbett), and then with Mary's coaching, perseverance, and utter confidence, he earns a spot with the leading team in the league, The Bears.

With the exception of Mary, no one is more proud to see Johnny become a success than Father O'Hara (Pat O'Brien), who has followed Johnny's career since he left the orphanage. But the Father's happiness is diminished as Johnny suffers increasingly from a swelled head; his egotism and harshness—even for a rough contact sport—alienates his teammates, and instead of resting up, "The Fireball" spends his evenings at parties with skating groupies like Polly (Marilyn).

Johnny's life is drastically altered when he contracts polio. The faithful Mary is there to see him through until he is well again and ready to return to the track. On the night of his comeback, Johnny unselfishly helps an up-and-coming teammate lead The Bears to the championship. Johnny celebrates with his most devoted allies, Mary and Father O'Hara.

GLENN CORBETT, MARILYN, JAMES BROWN, AND MICKEY ROONEY, RINKSIDE.

Act Two: *Foxiest Starlet*

"I can see your career rising in the east, like the sun."

—Addison DeWitt to Marilyn as Miss Caswell in *All About Eve*

Young Marilyn had influential friends who believed in her and were as anxious to see her in substantial roles as she was to play them. Her devoted agent, Johnny Hyde, negotiated Marilyn into MGM's *The Asphalt Jungle*. With the impression she made in that film and Hyde's backing, she had the clout to get back to Fox. During the next two years she worked there and at other studios in roles of increasing size that were stepping stones in her ascent to stardom.

At Fox in 1951–52 Marilyn helped bring attention to a fortunate group of films, mostly comedies. They were low-key, and although classified as B pictures, they were made in the studio era at one of the major movie companies, where top directors, cinematographers, and technicians in every field were employed, putting forth their talent into all of the studio's output, so that even B pictures had a polished look.

Marilyn never sneered at her early succession of frivolous blonde roles. She relished each new experience. They could all be described as "small but showy," not because they were inherently so, but because Marilyn made them interesting. The camera lingers on her for what she imparted to these films. Beyond the humor—and she was indeed terribly funny—there was undeniably an effortless sex appeal that radiated from her. Because without Marilyn's presence this element was otherwise missing from many of her early movies, she was frequently a key player in the promotion, regardless of the amount of screen time she actually had.

MARILYN

···In Fast Company·

Johnny Hyde, one of the best agents in the business, sold Zanuck on the idea of bringing Marilyn back into the Fox family in the spring of 1950 to appear in *All About Eve*. Hyde also convinced Marilyn of the value of taking a small part in a prestigious picture. A standout performance in such a film could make the public as well as other producers take notice of her. Furthermore, she would be working for Joseph L. Mankiewicz, a distinguished director whose body of work proved he was especially proficient with actresses. Marilyn had just demonstrated in *The Asphalt Jungle* that she could ably hold her own alongside experienced performers in a minor, but (in the hands of Marilyn) attention-grabbing part.

The cast, consisting of mostly veteran performers, included Bette Davis, Anne Baxter, George Sanders, Celeste Holm, Gary Merrill, Hugh Marlowe, Gregory Ratoff, and Thelma Ritter. In spite of her career being on the rise, Celeste Holm commented, "[Marilyn] seemed to be a lost, lonely little girl." She left much the same impression on Mankiewicz. More often alone than mixing with the company, the director found her studying Rainer Maria Rilke's *Letters to a Young Poet* during filming.

Marilyn acted in two sequences in *All About Eve*. One was a party, which was shot at Fox and for which wardrobe director Charles Le Maire had a gown made up specifically for Marilyn. For her other scene, she flew to San Francisco with cast and crew members to film at the Curran Theater.

READY TO FILM THE MEMORABLE STAIRCASE SCENE AT THE PARTY.
MARILYN IS SEEN WITH ANNE BAXTER, GARY MERRILL, GEORGE SANDERS, AND CELESTE HOLM.

Margo Channing:

"You're in a beehive, pal.
Didn't you know?
We're all busy little bees, full of stings,
making honey day and night.
Aren't we, honey?"

MARILYN IN 1950, THE SUBJECT OF FOX STILL PHOTOGRAPHER
FRANK POWOLNY'S CAMERA.

THEATER FOLK TALK SHOP AS MISS CASWELL ABSORBS SERENELY.

"Fasten your seat belts. It's going to be a bumpy night."

Broadway's leading actress, Margo Channing (Bette Davis), who has reached the sensitive age of forty, meets her greatest fan in Eve Harrington (Anne Baxter), a stage-struck girl who haunts the theater night after night. Eve's hard-luck story gives her the semblance of a helpless soul. Margo, not usually inclined to such gestures, takes her in. While Eve is efficient and willing to do anything for Margo, "the honeymoon is on." Soon however, Margo becomes aware that Eve will do anything to usurp her position in the theater, including befriending, using, and then discarding anyone who can help her climb the next step. Among her targets are Margo's fiancé, director Bill Sampson (Gary Merrill); her influential best friend, Karen Richards (Celeste Holm); and Karen's playwright husband, Lloyd Richards (Hugh Marlowe). Although they come to realize what a devious person Eve is, no one can slow her meteoric rise in the theater, with the possible exception of the acid-tongued commentator Addison DeWitt (George Sanders), and Phoebe (Barbara Bates), Eve's very own young and exceedingly devoted number-one fan.

As Claudia Caswell

As Claudia Caswell

"Miss Caswell is an actress. A graduate of the Copacabana School of Dramatic Art."

Specialized Courses from the Copacabana

Cultivate influential friends: Columnist Addison DeWitt, producer Max Fabian

Hobnob with the theatrical elite: he leading actress of the stage is the perfect opportunity to see and be seen by present and future leading lights of the show world.

Play it cool and drop a few pearls of wisdom: Miss Caswell says just enough to keep the people intrigued.

Dress to impress: Immaculately groomed (Marilyn's hair styled as it never was before or after) and wearing a strapless gown and ermine cape well beyond the means of the average aspiring actress, she arrives on the arm of Addison DeWitt.

Postgraduate Studies: Claudia Caswell is a new actress. Something she apparently never learned was how to steady her nerves for an important audition, which she follows with an unseemly haste to the ladies' room. She considers a new medium:

"Tell me this. Do they have auditions for television?"

Addison: "That's all television is, my dear. Nothing but auditions."

A Wise Soul

Sensitive and perceptive if one pauses to take in her words, rather like Lorelei Lee, Miss Caswell may be a girl of unsuspected depth . . .

Miss Caswell: *"Oh waiter."*

Addison: *"That isn't a waiter, my dear. That's a butler."*

Miss Caswell: *"Well I can't yell, 'Oh butler', can I?" Maybe somebody's name is Butler."*

Addison: *"You have a point. An idiotic one, but a point."*

Miss Caswell: *"I don't want to make trouble. All I want is a drink."*

Max Fabian: *"Leave it to me . . . I'll get you one."*

Miss Caswell: *"Thank you, Mr. Fabian."*

On producers:

Miss Caswell: *"Why do they always look like unhappy rabbits?"*

Addison: *"Because that's what they are. Now go and make him happier."*

With a glint in her eyes, she saunters off to do just that. We soon find out how she fared: She talked Max Fabian into allowing her to audition for the part of Margo's sister in *Aged in Wood*.

LIKE THE ACTRESS HERSELF, MISS CASWELL PROJECTED A UNIQUELY ALLURING BRAND OF VULNERABILITY AND SURPRISED THOSE FORTUNATE TO BE NEAR HER WITH HER OBSERVATIONS ON LIFE.

Eve vs. Miss Caswell

In a subtle way, Addison's protégé is juxtaposed against Margo's, starting with the contrast in their appearance—Eve wears a pretty but plain dress compared to Miss Caswell's designer gown and furs. Both are ambitious and know tricks to achieve their goals and both convey a certain helpless quality that gives others the impetus to help them. We know, in the manipulative Eve at least, that it is a front. The scene that takes place in the theater illustrates the chasm between the two aspiring actresses as Eve steals the spotlight during Miss Caswell's tryout. From the stomach-turning reaction that takes Miss Caswell by surprise, it was presumably her first audition. She has neither the talent nor the nerve of Eve. The winner in the audition takes Addison as well, as he transfers his attention from Miss Caswell to Eve.

Another actress wears a full-length sable coat to Margo's party. The censors objected to the first line of the following dialogue, but Mankiewicz kept it in.

Miss Caswell:	*"Now there's something a girl could make sacrifices for."*
Bill Sampson:	*"And probably has."*
Miss Caswell:	*"Sable"*
Max Fabian:	*"Sable? Did she say sable or Gable?"*
Miss Caswell:	*"Either one."*

Record-Breaker

Entire books have been written on the subject of *All About Eve*. A film whose working title was appropriately enough *Best Performance*, it showed excellence in every department. Being a part of this company, Marilyn got to bask in its reflected glory. She presented one of the eleven Academy Awards the film won, for sound recording, to Thomas Moulton. Among the other wins were Best Picture and Best Director.

All About Eve earned an unprecedented fourteen Oscar nominations. This record was held until 1997, when it was tied by *Titanic* (the latter, however, was nominated in some categories that did not exist in 1950). Mankiewicz's screenplay was based on Mary Orr's short story "The Wisdom of Eve," which appeared in *Cosmopolitan* magazine. His brilliantly witty adaptation excelled on multiple levels so that it was nominated in both the categories of best drama and best comedy writing by the Writers Guild of America. (It won for comedy.)

MARILYN GETS SPECIAL ATTENTION FROM DIRECTOR JOSEPH MANKIEWICZ.

··· *Young at Heart* ·

As Young as You Feel are words to live by for John Hodges (Monty Woolley), a faithful employee at Acme Printing Services who does not intend to accept an enforced retirement from the job he loves in the hand press department simply because he has reached a certain age. John has a brainstorm to change company policy by impersonating Harold P. Cleveland (Minor Watson), the elusive president of Acme's parent company, Consolidated Motors. During a visit to Acme, "Cleveland" tells off the boss, Mr. McKinley (Albert Dekker), saying that their retirement policy is asinine. The policy revoked, John thinks he can slip quietly out of his disguise, until a luncheon is given in his honor, at which he is obliged to make a speech. His views on American business are praised in newspapers and soon "Cleveland" is a national hero. Near-chaos ensues. John's family is in a dither, from his son, George (Allyn Joslyn), to off-kilter daughter-in-law Della (Thelma Ritter), to granddaughter Alice (Jean Peters) and her fiancé, Joe (David Wayne). In addition, John's youthful spirit and affinity for rumba dancing puts the McKinley marriage on the rocks as Mrs. McKinley (Constance Bennett) decides she is in love with John. McKinley takes his anger out on his poor secretary, Harriet (Marilyn). The real Harold P. Cleveland cannot afford to deny having made the widely praised speech. Furthermore, he agrees with every word. Inevitably, Cleveland lands on the Hodges' doorstep. During his visit, all is explained, peace is restored, and John is left able to happily step out of the spotlight, back to his old hand press at Acme.

MARILYN AS HARRIET, WITH ALBERT DEKKER AS BOSS LOUIS MCKINLEY.

Johnny's Final Act

Marilyn was given a new six-month, $500 per week contract with Fox on December 10, 1950. It was Johnny Hyde's last professional action on her behalf. Her agent died eight days after the contract went into effect as Marilyn worked on her role of Harriet in *As Young as You Feel*. Never one to let her personal troubles reflect on the screen, she cleverly played up the comedy bits Lamar Trotti wrote into his script for her. Sensing Marilyn's value to the film, they had her character pop up often, even to just cross the hall and say nothing.

Although this featherweight comedy was Harmon Jones's first directing job, he was an experienced editor with credits including *Scudda Hoo! Scudda Hay*! and *A Ticket to Tomahawk. Will You Love Me in December?* was his working title for *As Young as You Feel*. With no standout box office names to feature, Marilyn got to share billing above the title with Monty Woolley, Thelma Ritter, David Wayne, Jean Peters, Constance Bennett, and four other cast members. Her name placed sixth on the list.

THE ADVERTISEMENTS SAID, "YOU'LL SNEAK A THOUSAND WOLF WHISTLES AT HARRIET."

Making Impressions

As Young as You Feel reached theaters in August 1951. In its review, the *New York Times* said, "This unpretentious little picture, which Lamar Trotti has written and produced, and which Harmon Jones has directed in a deliciously nimble style, is a vastly superior entertainment. . . . Marilyn Monroe is superb . . ."

HARRIET IS QUITE TAKEN WITH THE OLD GENTLEMAN. THE ELOQUENCE OF "MR. CLEVELAND" LEAVES HER BESOTTED.

HARRIET IS QUESTIONED ABOUT MR. CLEVELAND . . .

Reporter: "Did you meet him Miss?"

Harriet: "Meet him? I took dictation from him."

"You know as a rule I never mix business with pleasure."

• Sexy and Efficient •

Harriet, a blonde bombshell of a secretary to the moody Mr. McKinley is also competent, organized, and not at all interested in dating the boss. When McKinley arrives in the mornings, she brings the mail to his office, recites his daily agenda, and pours his coffee. Alas, her efficiency cannot keep the boss from making subtle passes. Dining out with his wife, McKinley encounters Harriet stepping out with Mr. Gallagher, the head of his personnel department. Both offenders know their boss has designs on Harriet and they make a beeline for the exit. McKinley is furious—she always declined his invitations to "business" dinners! This, coupled with his elegant wife's newfound interest in an amiable older gentleman, makes him belligerent at the office. Poor Harriet is thrown for a loop, causing her to lose her usual poise and make faces behind McKinley's back.

HARRIET, THE PROFICIENT SECRETARY, KEEPS WELL-SUPPLIED WITH PENCILS WHEN TAKING DICTATION FROM MCKINLEY, WHO APPEARS NOT TO CARE HOW HIS WORDS ARE RECORDED AS LONG AS HE CAN BE NEAR HARRIET WHEN HE SPEAKS THEM.

"Mr. McKinley control yourself!"

"Go fry an egg!"

"Well!"

On the town with Wally Brown, Marilyn's Harriet is spotted dining out at a country club with the personnel manager. Meanwhile at the same club, *Mrs.* McKinley spends the evening on the dance floor with another man. Next day at the office, McKinley loses control and Harriet absorbs the brunt of it, though not without losing her own composure.

A Momentous Meeting

As one major player left Marilyn's life, another entered. She met Arthur Miller during the making of *As Young as You Feel*. Elia Kazan, with whom Marilyn was romantically linked in this period, was a friend of Miller's and director Harmon Jones. When Miller was in town Kazan brought him to the set of *As Young as You Feel* to meet Marilyn and Jones. At the moment Marilyn was not available for introductions. She was, as she had been found other times during this production, off by herself crying over the passing of Johnny Hyde. Marilyn and Miller were charmed by each other when they got to meet properly and talk at length at a party a short time later.

HARRIET GLOWS AT THE SOUND OF THE VOICE ON THE OTHER END OF THE LINE. LIKEWISE, MARILYN MET THE MAN SHE LOVED TALKING TO BEST DURING THE MAKING OF *AS YOUNG AS YOU FEEL*.

···A WAC in His Life

The above, one of several working titles for *Love Nest*, and the actresses suggested for the role of Roberta, indicate a greater emphasis on the character in early stages. Among those Fox considered offering the part to were Lauren Bacall, Marilyn, Jean Peters, Lucille Ball, and Helene Stanley (the memorable dancing teenager of the diner in *The Asphalt Jungle*). Marilyn at this stage was the obvious choice to add spice to the movie. Records show that William Holden and Anne Baxter were the first choices for the lead roles, which went to June Haver and William Lundigan.

Love Nest was adapted from a novel by Scott Corbett called *The Reluctant Landlord.* The author's original title was retained for the film project for a short time and then promptly changed to *A WAC in His Life*, then *The Love Nest*, before *Love Nest* was finally settled on. Marilyn contributed her signature sex appeal to the proceedings under the direction of Joseph Newman. Along with Marilyn, one-time vaudeville headliner Frank Fay was a highlight in the film, playing a charmingly deceptive character that must have been a comic spin on Uncle Charlie, the Merry Widow Murderer of Alfred Hitchcock's *Shadow of a Doubt*.

WITH JUNE HAVER AND WILLIAM LUNDIGAN

37

"The Screen's Most Heartwarming Housewarming"

Jim Scott (William Lundigan) returns from military service to his wife, Connie (June Haver), and the quaint love nest she has picked out for them: an apartment house cursed with an assortment of problems that add up to one large, expensive headache. Besides the wiring and plumbing that need fixing, there are tenants to keep happy, among them Roberta, or "Bobbi," a curvaceous old army chum of Jim's, and Charley Patterson (Frank Fay), a model of gentility but a highly suspicious character. When an FBI agent turns up, Jim and Connie find out that charming Charley has been swindling wealthy widows. Charley truly falls in love with his fellow tenant, a poor widow with nothing but love to offer, Eadie Gaynor (Leatrice Joy). Connie is greatly concerned about the romance, fearing Eadie will be hurt. The Scotts, however, have their own problems—their building is on the verge of being condemned and they can't afford the cost of repairs. Soon the FBI men come for Charley. From behind bars, Charley gives the story of his life to Jim to turn into a bestselling novel. The royalties roll in and the Scotts' apartment house is brought up to code. Charley, who never actually harmed anyone, is able to marry Eadie upon his release from prison. In the end, the Pattersons' happiness mirrors that of Jim and Connie's in their idyllic love nest.

JIM SHOWS ROBERTA UP TO HER APARTMENT.

LANDLORDS AND TENANTS

Jim tries, feebly, to talk Connie out of her reluctance to let Roberta move into their last vacant apartment.

"Well, you wouldn't discriminate against a veteran just because of SEX, would you?"

THE ETERNAL TRIANGLE

Corporal Stevens

Jim has told his wife about Corporal Stevens, an old army buddy he was stationed with in Paris, to whom he owes a debt of gratitude for coaxing their colonel into getting his discharge from service sooner than planned. But "Bobbi" turns out to be Roberta, quite possibly the Army's sexiest soldier. She puts Connie on the defensive from the first by catching Connie in work clothes and mistaking her for the janitor's wife. As a WAC, Roberta was a colonel's driver. In civilian life she is a friendly, fun-loving fashion model. Usually smartly dressed as becomes a girl of her profession, she is also perfectly comfortable sunbathing in a two-piece polka dot swimsuit, ogled by Jim's best friend (played by Jack Paar) while Jim does a bit of landscaping.

MARILYN AWAITS HER CUE ON THE *LOVE NEST* SET.

For the filming of this scene, which began attracting more crew members than was necessary, director Joseph Newman had to bar people from the set.

· As Roberta Stevens ·

As Roberta Stevens

"Seems strange giving money to a man you know."

A Word from the Censors...

The Hollywood film industry's censorship board, commonly called the Hays Office, reviewed all screenplays to ensure strict adherence to the Production Code by the studios. The censors had no objections to Roberta. The script was submitted for review at the regular intervals but it was impossible to tell how coquettish the character could be when played by Marilyn. What the censors did find crude were references to a toilet in comic dialogue between Jim and Connie about the building's plumbing problems. These lines were cut from the script.

A Wife's Suspicion is Piqued . . .

Roberta: "You know, all the time we were overseas Jim talked of nothing but you."

Connie: "You must have found that pretty dull."

Roberta: "Oh no, Jim can make anything interesting."

MARILYN AS THE ROMANTIC ROBERTA PLAYED OPPOSITE JACK PAAR. THE ACTOR WAS A FEW YEARS AWAY FROM STARDOM AS HOST OF HIS OWN POPULAR LATE-NIGHT TV SHOW.

Diamond Partnership

Love Nest marked the entrance of I. A. L. Diamond into Marilyn's professional life. This light post-World War II comedy, while not the best, was the first of four scripts he wrote for Marilyn, and his first for Fox after five years at Warner Bros. At both studios he penned a number of enjoyable comedies, but he was at his best when partnered with Billy Wilder, with whom he wrote *Love in the Afternoon*, *The Apartment*, and *Some Like it Hot*, among a number of brilliant screenplays.

Diamond wrote in a playful scene for Marilyn with no dialogue in which Roberta spots her old friend Jim sleeping on her couch as she prepares to take a shower. She merrily continues undressing as Jim carries on with his nap.

IMAGES FROM CONTACT SHEET OF THE FILMING OF ROBERTA'S PARTY · A SCENE THAT DID NOT MAKE IT INTO THE FINAL PRINT.

··· Making it Legal ·

Just as Marilyn was going to work on Let's Make it Legal, her latest six-month contract was expiring. Fox was quick to set before her a new agreement, signed on May 11, 1951, this one for seven years. Darryl Zanuck knew that in Marilyn his studio had something special—he seemed doubtful this something was an actress, but he knew she had a quality audiences responded to. She was an electrifying personality and could enhance any film in which she turned up. In May 1951, the latest comedy in need of that extra something was *Let's Make it Legal*.

This time the stars were Claudette Colbert and Macdonald Carey. Young actors on the rise along with Marilyn were the handsome Robert Wagner (with whom she made two screen tests), and Barbara Bates (*All About Eve*'s Phoebe). Richard Sale, who had directed her in *A Ticket to Tomahawk*, was the film's director. Again the script was by I. A. L. Diamond, this time in collaboration with F. Hugh Herbert.

MARILYN ADJUSTS HER COSTUME BETWEEN TAKES WITH MACDONALD CAREY.

Gambling on Love

Miriam Halworth's (Claudette Colbert) love for husband Hugh (Macdonald Carey) is dispelled by his penchant for gambling. She wants a divorce. Hugh still loves her, and the arrival in town of Miriam's old flame, the slimy, successful politician Victor Macfarland (Zachary Scott) arouses his ire (and the fervor of a certain young model—Marilyn). Victor does not mean a thing to Miriam anymore, but when Hugh bets her $20 that she cannot "hook" him, Miriam sets out to bring the confirmed bachelor to his knees—or at least one knee, with a ring in his hand.

Daughter Barbara (Barbara Bates) is determined to get her parents back together, even as her husband Jerry (Robert Wagner) is anxious to see Miriam settled with either one of the two men, so long as his wife will start acting like a grown woman instead of a child. Barbara tries to play up the fact that Miriam is a grandmother, but Victor is not dissuaded. He asks Miriam to be his wife. She accepts his proposal and is about to follow her senatorial candidate fiancé to Washington when some of Hugh's screwball antics land Miriam, Barbara, Jerry, and Hugh in a police station, and subsequently splashed across the newspapers. Victor's great fear of a scandal brings out the fact that Miriam means much less to him than his career does. It also shows Miriam how much she loves Hugh, flaws and all.

JOYCE CHASES HER MILLIONAIRE OF CHOICE TO THE GOLF COURSE, BUT HAS TO SETTLE FOR HUGH INSTEAD AS MACFARLAND MAKES A HASTY RETREAT WITH MIRIAM.

Miss Cucamonga

Joyce Mannering, a model recently named Miss Cucamonga, has her gold-digging heart set on millionaire Victor Macfarland, but he is immune to her charms, preferring the company of Miriam, the ex-sweetheart he lost to another man in a game of craps. Even in a form-fitting strapless evening dress, Joyce literally has to be thrown at Victor to get his attention. While waiting for Victor to come around, she can most likely be found posing for cheesecake photos by the pool at Hugh's Hotel Miramar. Joyce knows how to be one of the guys too. She keeps Hugh and his friends company while they play poker and is even up for a round herself. Surely if she can't turn Victor's head, any one of Joyce's poker buddies would be willing to take her out.

"Honey, your father's been so divine with me that sometimes even I feel like calling him 'Daddy.'"

"Who wouldn't want to meet a man worth millions who isn't even bald?"

JOYCE PLEADS FOR AN INTRODUCTION TO A POT OF GOLD NAMED MACFARLAND—WHO PROVES VERY
DIFFICULT TO CATCH UP WITH, LEAVING HER UTTERLY FRUSTRATED.

"My motor's been racing since I first laid eyes on him."

"What happened to that vibrating motor of yours?"

"He turned off the ignition."

YOUNG MARILYN, SLIGHTLY RESEMBLING GRACE KELLY IN THIS SHOT, WITH MACDONALD CAREY.
THE FILM'S WORKING TITLE WAS *DON'T CALL ME MOTHER*, A REFERENCE, OF COURSE,
NOT TO MARILYN, BUT TO CLAUDETTE COLBERT'S POSITION IN THE FILM AS A YOUTHFUL GRANDMOTHER.

MARILYN ENJOYED HER EARLY ROLES, AS THIS PHOTO FROM THE SET OF *LET'S MAKE IT LEGAL* SHOWS, BUT EVEN AT THIS STAGE,
SHE LONGED TO PLAY ROLES THAT REQUIRED MORE THAN PERFECT MAKEUP.

Taking it Seriously

Marilyn well understood the value of publicity, and she was attracting more than her fair share in the advertising of her comedies. As her roles began to expand, she wanted to be better. Aware that sex appeal did not make a great actress, Marilyn worked hard to improve as an actress. She had studied at the Actor's Lab between 1947 and 1949, and now began working with Michael Chekov (who honed his craft with the "father of modern theatre," Stanislavski), in addition to her personal coach, Natasha Lytess, with whom she had been studying since 1948, for Columbia's *Ladies of the Chorus.*

Now sought by other studios as well, Marilyn went from Fox's frothy *Let's Make it Legal* to the dramatic *Clash by Night* for RKO Pictures in the fall of 1951. Producer Jerry Wald negotiated a loan-out from Fox for her to appear in an adaptation of the Clifford Odets play. In *Clash by Night* she gave her best acting performance to date and earned commendable reviews.

···The Grand Motif

While Marilyn was on loan to RKO, the omnibus production *We're Not Married* was being prepared at Fox. With many slots to fill in the all-star, episodic production, the natural thought was, *Get Marilyn in there—preferably in a swimsuit!* Writer-producer Nunnally Johnson came up with the part of a beauty pageant winner for Marilyn. In this role she played a mother for the first time, though she never interacts with the child. Among the other stars appearing in various vignettes in *We're Not Married* were Ginger Rogers, Fred Allen, Paul Douglas, Eve Arden, Donald O'Connor, Mitzi Gaynor, Louis Calhern, and Zsa Zsa Gabor. All were directed by Edmund Goulding, who had experience handling a high-profile cast dating back to *Grand Hotel* (1932), which was one of, if not the, first of Hollywood's prestigious all-star features.

"You mean it means . . . we're not married anymore?"
"Darling! How wonderful!"

MARILYN IS SEWN INTO HER COSTUME.

READY FOR THE CAMERA WITH A FEW FINAL ADJUSTMENTS.

ANNABEL KEEPS AN EYE ON HER BABY WHILE WAITING FOR THE CUE TO SAY "I DO" THE SECOND TIME AROUND.

If you had it to do over . . .

Dizzy Justice of the Peace Melvin Bush (Victor Moore) jumped the gun and began marrying couples before the official date of his appointment. As a result, none of the couples are legally wed. Each pair is notified of the mistake and now it is up to them to decide if they want to remarry, or if now given a second chance, they would choose *un*married bliss.

Among those affected by Bush's blunder are Mr. and Mrs. Jefferson D. Norris. Annabel Norris (Marilyn) is a professional beauty pageant contestant and Jeff (David Wayne) must remain in the background to mind the baby and take care of the house-work. With the help of her sharpshooter agent (James Gleason), Annabel is on her way to becoming Mrs. America. The prospect of winning leads to talk of Annabel traveling across the globe for film, radio, and nightclub spots. At this point Jeff happily breaks the news that she is no longer eligible to compete for the Mrs. title in any contest, because they are not actually married. Very soon after, Jeff is found proudly whistling from the audience as his *fiancée* is crowned *Miss* Mississippi.

GETTING A TROPHY AND HER PIC-
TURE IN THE PAPERS IS GOOD, BUT
ANNABEL LEARNS THE REAL
PRIZES GO TO MISS MISSISSIPPI.

~~Mrs. Senatobia~~
no, no—
Miss Mississippi

Recalled by Justice Bush as a shy young girl, Mrs. Norris grew up and shed her inhibitions to become a beauty queen known professionally as Mrs. Senatobia, or more recently, Mrs. Mississippi. Annabel Norris is in private life a young mother and wife to henpecked husband Jeff, who is floored by her unflatteringly joyous reaction to the news that she is legally still unwed Annabel Jones. To her, the thrilling part is this qualifies her to become *Miss* Mississippi, a far more desirable title accorded first-class treatment and greater monetary support from local businesses than her Mrs. counterpart. Annabel may be one-track-minded on the surface, but she does in fact remarry Jeff, and once her professional goals are achieved, she may even consider becoming a full-time wife and mother.

MARILYN SHOWS THE TWO SIDES OF ANNABEL. THE BEAUTY CONTEST QUEEN IN A PUBLICITY STILL (TOP) AND SERENE AS THE BRIDE BACKSTAGE (LEFT).

STATE FINALS
BATHING BEAUTY CONTEST

THE CROWD APPLAUDS THEIR FAVORITE BATHING BEAUTY.

Husband and Spectator

Jeff:	*"Like her?"*
Man in Audience:	*"Boy, that's really something."*
Jeff:	*"My wife."*
Man:	*"Oh. Beg your pardon."*
Jeff:	*"Oh that's alright, keep looking."*
Man:	*"Much obliged."*

*"Go ahead and look.
I gotta get used to it sooner or later."*

Marilyn and David

Marilyn's most frequent co-star was none other than David Wayne, with whom she shared four film credits, though they only played opposite each other twice. Perhaps not a match made in heaven, they were cute together. For a time, Fox planned to cast him as Gus Esmond in *Gentlemen Prefer Blondes*. Wayne never acted over-awed by her looks. In appearance he was boyish to her bombshell exterior; in heels she was taller than the 5' 7" actor. He had to know that all eyes were on Marilyn, yet he came across relaxed and un-intimidated.

Wayne acted in a number of films, but the bulk of his work could be seen on television and the stage. He was an acclaimed Broadway actor, and by the time he teamed up with Marilyn, he had already won his first Tony for *Finian's Rainbow*.

Monroe–Wayne Films:
As Young as You Feel
We're Not Married
O. Henry's Full House
How to Marry a Millionaire

JEFF IS STUNNED BY ANNABEL'S REACTION TO THE NEWS THAT THEY ARE NOT MARRIED.

Staying Occupied

Marilyn was known to cause long waits on her sets, but there were always many reasons for the extended breaks between actual filming typical on a movie set, mostly for camera and lighting setups, which could take hours. During her own frequent waits, Marilyn used the downtime well.

BEING LETTER PERFECT BY STUDYING THE SCRIPT WAS IDEAL.

KEEPING HERSELF PICTURE PERFECT WAS ESSENTIAL.

MARILYN ALWAYS LOVED TALKING ON THE TELEPHONE.

MARILYN IS PREPARED FOR HER TENSE FINAL SCENE.

MARILYN HAD TO SHOW THE ARRAY OF EMOTIONS THAT TORMENTED HER CHARACTER IN *DON'T BOTHER TO KNOCK*.

ENCOUNTERING A LOCKED DOOR, NELL
NERED IN THE LOBBY OF THE HOTEL. W
RAZOR BLADE IN HAND, EXTREME CAU
NECESSARY IN APPROACHING HER.

· · · Greatest Challenge Yet

Marilyn's notoriety and popularity with the public was increasing dramatically. Her first starring role at Fox, and the most unusual the studio ever gave her, came in early 1952 with *Don't Bother to Knock*. Having recently played against type as a cannery worker on the San Francisco waterfront in RKO's *Clash by Night*, she would now bring to life Nell, a psychotic young woman left to care for an unsuspecting child. Marilyn's ever-increasing concentration on her acting studies showed. She had earned her chance to try something new. Three years before she began studying Method acting with Lee Strasberg, her performance here demonstrates the raw talent that was present early on. Marilyn did a fine job of making the audience empathize with Nell, conveying different levels of inner tension. She is quite touching, perhaps drawing on memories of her mother, who suffered from mental illness and had to be institutionalized when Marilyn was eight years old. Throughout adulthood, the fear of ending up the same way was a persistent source of anxiety, so playing a mentally ill woman must have been an ordeal for her.

MARILYN IS FIRST INTRODUCED TO LITTLE DONNA CORCORAN AND HER PARENTS IN THE FILM, PLAYED BY JIM BACKUS AND LURENE TUTTLE. LITTLE DO THEY KNOW WHAT THEY'RE IN FOR WHEN NELL TAKES CHARGE.

THE POLICE COME FOR THE SUICIDAL NELL IN THIS SCENE PLAYED OUT BY MARILYN, ANNE BANCROFT, RICHARD WIDMARK, AND CHARLES FLYNN.

Casting Calls

Nell Forbes: The simple description of Nell was, "The leading lady—a girl in her 20s, attractive, fresh with an innocent air about her."

Casting suggestions: Anne Baxter, Jennifer Jones, Marilyn Monroe, Jean Peters, Shirley Temple, and Elizabeth Taylor

Jed Towers: Richard Widmark, Montgomery Clift, Joseph Cotten, and Victor Mature

Eddie Forbes: Described as, "Little wrinkled man about 50. Nervous type. Elevator operator." Sound like a description of Elisha Cook, Jr.? They had in mind Richard Taber or Everett Sloane.

A SCENE WITH RICHARD WIDMARK AND ELISHA COOK, JR. JED NURSES EDDIE, WHO HAS BEEN INJURED BY NELL, AND WONDERS WHAT SHE WILL DO NEXT.

MARILYN LISTENS INTENTLY IN PREPARATION FOR A SCENE.

One Take Wonder

Based on a novel by Charlotte Armstrong, working titles for the picture were *Mischief* (after Armstrong's novel) and *Night Without Sleep*. The television remake in 1990 had yet another name, *The Sitter*. Marilyn was paid her standard $500 per week for *Don't Bother to Knock*, as was Anne Bancroft (then still Anne Marno), who was making her film debut. Richard Widmark earned a $1,750 weekly stipend. Marilyn had a strong supporting cast, along with British director Roy Baker, to bring out her best. Baker tried to make up for budget constraints by insisting on printing the first take, which only proves further what a remarkable task this was for Marilyn, an actress whose necessity for numerous takes would become a signature characteristic.

READY TO FILM

ON THE SET DURING REHEARSALS

"And please, don't get into anymore mischief."

Recently discharged from a mental institution in Oregon, Nell Forbes comes to New York to settle in new surroundings. Her well-meaning Uncle Eddie (Elisha Cook, Jr.) arranges a babysitting job for her in the hotel where he is employed as an elevator operator. Alone in the hotel room with Bunny Jones (Donna Corcoran), Nell puts the child to bed. She then plays dress-up with Mrs. Jones's best negligee, spots the handsome man across the courtyard, and the mischief begins.

The cynical Jed is on the rebound from nightclub singer Lyn Lesley (Anne Bancroft). He is a nice enough man but lacks the heart Lyn wants in a husband. Hoping Nell can make him forget his troubles, Jed goes across the way to spend the evening in her room. Catching Nell in lie after lie, he finds out that she is a very disturbed woman. Because he is a pilot, Nell begins to confuse Jed with her dead fiancé, Philip, whose disappearance after a plane crash in the Pacific led to her mental breakdown.

Jed's initial reaction is to try to get out of Room 801. In Nell's mind, interruptions from Bunny and Eddie are to blame for scaring Jed off, and she takes drastic action to prevent their interference. Eddie is knocked out and Bunny is bound and gagged in her bedroom. Just as the authorities are called in, Nell's mind slips further into madness. Jed's growing concern for her is obvious, proving to Lyn that he is indeed a caring man. Nell is quietly taken away to prevent her from harming anyone, including herself. This time Nell is not alone. She has Jed and Lyn to see her through the darkness.

WITH ONE WELL-DIRECTED SWING OF AN ASHTRAY, NELL PUTS EDDIE'S LIGHTS OUT.

"MY DRESS IS TORN." THE ELEVATOR BOY KNOWS SOMETHING ISN'T RIGHT WITH HIS PASSENGER.

NELL WARNS THE LITTLE GIRL——SHE DOESN'T WANT TO HEAR A SOUND.

Nell: "Do you have a doll at home?"

Bunny: "Yes. Josephine."

Nell: "What if it cried and pestered and spied on you?
You'd want to get rid of it wouldn't you?
You'd have to."

Fragile after years in an institution, Nell's doctors have advised that a new setting would help in her recovery. That is why she is in New York with Uncle Eddie. She wants to show that she can handle the new job he has arranged for her, but Nell seems lost and apprehensive from the moment she enters the hotel. Once her charge is tucked in bed, Nell has nothing to do except admire the feminine frills belonging to Mrs. Jones. Nell arrived wearing a drab, wrinkled dress. She has worn nothing nicer in at least three years, and cannot help slipping on Mrs. Jones's fine negligee, as well as her stockings, earrings, perfume, and makeup, allowing her to play society girl for a time—a vision of delight both to Nell and the man in Room 821. Estranged from her abusive parents, Philip's death left her alone and suicidal. In her state of mind, Bunny's frequent intrusions of her tête-à-tête are more than enough to trigger Nell's violent tendencies, leading to an unforgettable night for everyone she encounters.

Beauty Transformation

There is an emotional transformation as well and Nell gets to play at being a carefree, wealthy socialite.

"I just wanted to see how they'd look on me for a while."

THIS BEHIND-THE-SCENES PHOTO SHOWS IT TOOK SEVERAL HANDS TO COMPLETE NELL'S BEAUTY TRANSFORMATION.

NELL BEGINS TO LIKE WHAT SHE SEES IN THE MIRROR.

THE NEW NELL

"You came over to flirt, didn't you?"

"I can't figure you out."
"You're silk on one side and sandpaper on the other."

. . .

"I'll be any way you want me to be."

SLIGHTLY OUT OF CHARACTER, THE REAL MARILYN, HAPPY TO HAVE HER FIRST SERIOUS ROLE,
SHINES THROUGH ON THE HOTEL LOBBY SET.

A PUBLICITY SHOT OF MARILYN AND WIDMARK SHOWING
NELL'S SILKY SIDE.

IT WAS THE CENSORS' JOB TO SEE THAT THE FILM WAS NOT QUITE AS SEXY AS THE ADVERTISEMENTS PROMISED.

You've never met her type before...
...a wicked sensation as the lonely girl in Room 809!

RICHARD **WIDMARK**
MARILYN **MONROE** in
Don't Bother to Knock

20th CENTURY-FOX

PRODUCED BY **JULIAN BLAUSTEIN** · DIRECTED BY **ROY BAKER** · SCREEN PLAY BY **DANIEL TARADASH** · BASED ON A NOVEL BY **CHARLOTTE ARMSTRONG**

A Word from the Censors...

There were Hays Office objections to the action of Nell dabbing perfume on the area of her chest.

Fighting among women must be handled with care, the censors instructed.

The Massachusetts censorship board deleted the scene in which Nell exposes her leg and displays her garters in the action of adjusting her stockings.

The wardrobe department was cautioned that Nell's negligee must not be revealing.

(LEFT) THE SCENE THE MASSACHUSETTS CENSORS ORDERED CUT.

THE CENSORS WERE CONCERNED ABOUT THE HAIR-PULLING FIGHT BETWEEN MARILYN AND LURENE TUTTLE, WHICH REMAINED IN THE FILM, BRIEFLY, AND WAS RECREATED WITH MORE VIOLENCE FOR PUBLICITY STILLS.

"The most talked about actress of 1952"

The tagline was not an exaggeration and with *Don't Bother to Knock*, Marilyn's contribution to the publicity campaign was finally analogous to the size of her role in the film. The reviews were mixed and it was not the financial success expected of a Marilyn Monroe starring vehicle, but she nevertheless would be cast in another major dramatic part later the same year.

> "Marilyn Monroe, co-starred with Richard Widmark, gives an excellent account of herself in a strictly dramatic role which commands certain attention . . . the studio has an upcoming dramatic star in Miss Monroe."
> —*Variety*

SPANISH-LANGUAGE LOBBY CARD FOR *DON'T BOTHER TO KNOCK*

GRAMMAR IS NOT LOIS LAUREL'S STRONG SUIT. AT LEAST SHE IS ADEPT AT FIELDING
THE MANY FRANTIC PHONE CALLS THAT COME IN FOR HER BOSS AT OXLY CHEMICAL.

"Good morning. Aren't you here early?"

"Oh yes, Mr. Oxly's been complaining about my
punctuation, so I'm careful to get here before nine."

···Hawksian Antics

Monkey Business was a revival of the screwball comedy genre that was at its peak in the mid- to late-1930s, made by some of the talents who first popularized the trend. Silly, nonsensical, it was the funniest of Marilyn's early comedies, as it should have been considering the people involved—Cary Grant, Ginger Rogers, Charles Coburn, director Howard Hawks, and screenwriters Charles Lederer, Ben Hecht, and I. A. L. Diamond. Though not the classic that might have emerged from such an assemblage, *Monkey Business* succeeded in engaging the audience in a world of unlikely situations played out by a very likeable team of fun-makers. What is unfortunate is that the film followed Marilyn's star turn in *Don't Bother to Knock*. Taking a step back from the lead position, she was playing another light-headed blonde secretary (albeit a thoroughly amusing one) and her screen time was limited.

THE BUSY CREW MEMBERS SET UP A SHOT, OBLIVIOUS TO THE GLAMOROUS CAMERAMAN IN THEIR MIDST.

Something in the Water

Chemist Barnaby Fulton (Cary Grant) is stumped by his latest experiment, a formula for restoring youth. Just as the idea seems hopeless, Esther, a lab monkey, gets loose from her cage and unbeknownst to any of the scientists, tosses together the ingredients in proportions that produce the very formula Barnaby was trying to achieve. Esther then pours her youth elixir into the water cooler, moments before Barnaby decides to test his own latest version of the mixture. He washes the dose down with a glass of water from the lab's now magic cooler. Soon Barnaby is behaving like a twenty-year-old, enjoying a day of youthful horseplay with Miss Laurel (Marilyn), the secretary of his boss at the chemical works, Mr. Oxly (Charles Coburn).

Lois: *"I've something to show you."*

Barnaby: *"For instance?"*

Lois: *"Isn't it wonderful?"*

Barnaby: *"I beg your pardon?"*

Lois: *"The new non-rip plastic stockings you invented."*

Mr. Oxly enters . . . *"Well, Miss Laurel was just showing me her acetates."*

LOIS: "THIS IS AN EXPERIMENTAL PAIR—THE FIRST PAIR OUT OF THE FACTORY. AREN'T YOU PROUD?"

BARNABY: "IT TURNED OUT RATHER WELL."

*"You're old only when you forget you're young. . . .
It's a word you keep in your heart. A light you have in your eyes . . .
Someone you hold in your arms."*

After the formula's effect on Barnaby wears off, Barnaby's wife, Edwina (Ginger Rogers) plays guinea pig next—also swallowing the dose with a drink of water. Within minutes Edwina turns into a dance-crazed bobbysoxer. Under the formula's influence, she panics on the night of her "second honeymoon," locks Barnaby out of their room, and takes steps toward obtaining a divorce via Barnaby's "rival," Hank Entwhistle (Hugh Marlowe).

By morning, Edwina has returned to normal, but soon the most dramatic turn yet with the spiked water occurs. Barnaby and Edwina revert to quarrelsome children. Barnaby plays Indian with the neighborhood kids and performs a scalping on Hank. Later Edwina becomes convinced that her husband has turned into the baby that mysteriously appears in their bedroom. Once both recover and the monkey's youth potion is disposed of, Barnaby couldn't be happier. The formula was nothing but trouble, and after all, you don't have to be young to feel young.

Oxly: "Find someone to type this."
Miss Laurel: "Oh Mr. Oxly, can't I try again?"
Oxly: "No, it's very important. Better find someone to type it for you. . . ."

MAYBE NEXT TIME OXLY WILL LET HER HAVE ANOTHER CRACK AT THE TYPEWRITER.

"Anybody Can Type"

. . . But how many secretaries can brighten an office like Miss Laurel? She is half infant, but as Edwina Fulton points out, certainly not the half that's visible. Lois Laurel is anxious to make a good secretary for boss Mr. Oxly, and is happy to test the chemical lab's practical experiments that do not involve magic potions, such as the non-rip plastic stockings invented by Barnaby.

The obvious playmate when Barnaby regresses to youth, she likes her music "hot," not sentimental, and when roller-skating, swimming, or joyriding, "young" Barnaby finds no one more fun to be with. She may have difficulty operating her typewriter, but Lois is not altogether senseless. She is, after all, the only one among a team of chemists who manages not to come under the influence of a monkey's science experiment.

PLAYING A SCENE WITH CARY GRANT AND CHARLES COBURN.

Battling Blondes

Round 1: Name calling

Edwina finds out whose lipstick is smeared on her husband's face. The mature woman, now reliving childish days of yesteryear calls out:

". . . you peroxide kissing-bug. I'll pull that blonde hair out by its black roots."

Round 2: Fight! Fight!

Soon Edwina turns violent at the sight of Lois.

"Put' em up—put' em up."

Round 3: Slingshot mischief

Between popping bubbles and snapping away at her chewing gum, Edwina takes pot shots at Lois's rear end with her slingshot, making Lois believe that Barnaby and Mr. Oxly, both standing beside her, are getting fresh.

"I did it. I fixed her! I shot her!"

Decision:

In favor of Miss Laurel, for being the only one able to maintain sanity in the midst of the wild goings-on.

EDWINA TRIES TO CONVINCE OXLY, LOIS, AND THE SCIENTISTS THAT HER HUSBAND HAS TURNED INTO AN INFANT.

LOIS, UNDERSTANDABLY, BECOMES TERRIFIED OF EDWINA.

THERE'S NOTHING LIKE A RIDE IN AN OPEN CAR.

On the Town with Barnaby and Lois

Car shopping

Barnaby trades in his old conservative car for a flashier model that appeals to his college-boy sensibilities—and to Lois.

Lois: "Is this your car? Gee, it's a honey."

Barnaby: "Well it takes one to know one."

Out for a spin

Barnaby takes Lois out for a joyride that starts off carefree, but turns increasingly frightening for her. Barnaby's youth serum wears off over the course of the day, bringing back the near-sightedness of his age. Finally they end in a head-on run-in with a fence outside of Oxly Chemical.

"Watch your head.
I'll watch everything else!"

Skating sensations

A day of youthful hijinks wouldn't be complete without a spin around the rink.

"Wait and see. I'll be good."

—*Barnaby*

"GOOD" MAY NOT BE THE WORD.

LACED UP AND READY FOR A WILD SPIN WITH CARY GRANT AS SOON
AS THE CAMERAS RESUME ROLLING.

ALL EYES ON LOIS

"Well, everybody looking at me?"

—*Barnaby*

By making the community swimming pool a stop during Lois and Barnaby's afternoon excursions, the screenwriters set up an excuse to display Marilyn in a swimsuit. Poor Barnaby's bid for attention—attempting swan dives—doesn't stand a chance.

LOIS CAN'T HELP STEALING THE SPOTLIGHT AT THE SWIMMING POOL.

CARY **GRANT** · GINGER **ROGERS** · CHARLES **COBURN** · MARILYN **MONROE**

in
HOWARD HAWKS'

monkey business

Darling I Am Growing Younger and *Be Your Age* were working titles for *Monkey Business*.

MARILYN POSED FOR ADVERTISEMENTS WITH A STAND-IN FOR CARY GRANT.

Barnaby: "Now say 'terrify.'"

Lois: "Terrify."

"Now say 'tissue.'"

"Tissue."

"Now say them both fast together."

"Terrifi-tissue?"

"No!"

Cary and Ginger who?

When three or more leading actors needed to be brought together to shoot what would become final poster art and other advertising materials for a film, it could be impossible to find a time that worked with everyone's busy schedules. Stand-ins could be employed to pose with the stars who were available. Later the faces of those missing would be set in place, usually successfully. Marilyn was under long-term contract to Fox. Though they made many films for the studio, Cary Grant and Ginger Rogers were not. And so Marilyn got to pose with the stand-ins.

THE RESULT OF HAVING THE PHOTOGRAPHS TURNED INTO ILLUSTRATIONS WERE NOT ALWAYS GREAT, AND SO MARILYN LOOKS MORE LIKE TERRY MOORE HERE.

Grand Marshal Marilyn

During an east coast publicity tour for *Monkey Business* in August/September 1952, Marilyn became the first woman elected to the honorary post of Grand Marshal at the Miss America pageant held in Atlantic City. She joyously waived to the crowd from an open car during a parade, wearing a dress cut down to her naval. The city also hosted the premiere of her latest film, and the marquee of the local theater upgraded her billing, advertising "Cary Grant and Marilyn Monroe in *Monkey Business*."

MARILYN PREPARES TO SHOOT THE SKATING SCENES. CARY GRANT'S STUNT DOUBLE CAN BE SEEN AT RIGHT.

An Eventful Spring

Monkey Business was filmed between March 5 and April 30, 1952. Off-screen in March, news coverage on Marilyn escalated to new heights as her famous "Golden Dreams" nude calendar surfaced. Instead of harming her career, as many predicted, her forthrightness in confirming the fact that she was indeed the model, and about the circumstances that led her to posing for the photos, only endeared her to the press and the public. America was completely hooked on Marilyn.

- Two days after the story of her nude photos broke, Marilyn met her future husband, baseball legend Joe DiMaggio. Their first date, arranged by a mutual friend, was also their first meeting. No conventional blind date, they hit it off and immediately began seeing each other regularly. DiMaggio's visit to the set of *Monkey Business* was highly publicized.

- The following month, Marilyn appeared on her first *Life* magazine cover, for the week of April 7, 1952.

- During filming, Marilyn suffered from strong abdominal pains that turned out to be appendicitis. She braved the aches until her work was completed and then went into the hospital for an appendectomy on May 6, 1952.

A RARE LOOK AT MARILYN IN THE CHEMICAL LAB OF THE MONKEY BUSINESS SET.

··· The O. Henry Twist ·

O. Henry's Full House placed Marilyn among a multitude of star names again for her cameo role. The picture, which had the working titles of *Baghdad on a Subway* and *Full House*, told a selection of stories by O. Henry, the pen name of American writer William Sydney Porter, whose exceedingly popular stories were famous for their unexpected endings. Enacted in the film are five favorite tales from O. Henry. Unlike *We're Not Married*, each story is an independent segment, employing five different sets of directors, stars, and writers. John Steinbeck acted as host to the stories.

Marilyn's segment, "The Cop and the Anthem," featured Charles Laughton in the lead, with David Wayne as his best buddy. Lamar Trotti wrote the dialogue and Henry Koster directed them. The other four stories were played out by Richard Widmark and Dale Robertson ("The Clarion Call"), Anne Baxter and Jean Peters ("The Last Leaf"), Fred Allen and Oscar Levant ("The Ransom of Red Chief"), and Jeanne Crain and Farley Granger ("The Gift of the Magi").

O. HENRY'S FULL HOUSE WAS ONE AMONG MANY ALL-STAR FEATURES MADE BY FOX IN THE '40S AND '50S. THEY WERE MADE POSSIBLE BY THE STUDIO SYSTEM AND PRODUCERS AT FOX LOVED TO TAKE ADVANTAGE OF THE OPPORTUNITY.

O. Henry's FULL HOUSE

FRED ALLEN ANNE BAXTER JEANNE CRAIN FARLEY GRANGER CHARLES LAUGHTON OSCAR LEVANT MARILYN MONROE JEAN PETERS GREGORY RATOFF DALE ROBERTSON DAVID WAYNE RICHARD WIDMARK

20th CENTURY FOX

The Cop and the Anthem

Soapy (Charles Laughton), a denizen of the streets of New York, is in the market for a well-heated spot as the winter cold sets in. While others dream of Florida, Soapy can think of nowhere he would rather spend the winter than the city jail, and the logical way to reserve a berth in this institution where beds are warm and the meals are regular, is to get arrested. Soapy knows a number of maneuvers to accomplish said mission, but the city dwellers have particularly warm hearts this day in spite of the weather. It seems there is no way for an earnest gentleman like Soapy to be hauled to jail. A kind restaurant owner lets him go without paying after feasting on the menu's priciest items; a well-groomed young lady (Marilyn) he tries to accost turns out to be amenable to the company of a smooth talker like Soapy. The dejected Soapy next stops at a church to regroup. There the singing of an angelic choir moves him deeply, inspiring Soapy to turn his life around and go to work. Standing outside of the church as he makes this vow to himself, Soapy's plans are put on hold—he is spotted by a policeman and arrested for loitering.

WITH CHARLES LAUGHTON. BOTH SOAPY AND THE GIRL ARE COMPLETELY MISTAKEN ABOUT EACH OTHER.

The Hobo and the Streetwalker

It is no ordinary young lady Soapy approaches in hopes that she will call out to the policeman standing nearby. In fact, in her mind she does not qualify as a lady at all. Embarrassed that he cannot follow through with his offer to buy her a drink, Soapy apologizes profusely for misleading her, offers her his sole possession (a fine umbrella) as a small token of his esteem with a few choice remarks, and proceeds on his way. The young woman is moved to tears by this encounter with a man of uncommon eloquence.

"Good afternoon my dear, aren't you a little lonely window shopping all by yourself? Wouldn't you prefer to come and play in my backyard?"

"Sure I don't mind if you buy me a drink."

Soapy: "My compliments to a charming and delightful young lady."

Policeman: "What's goin' on here? What's happenin'?"

Streetwalker: "He called me a lady."

THE LADY WATCHES A MEMORABLE CHARACTER WALK OUT OF HER LIFE.

Soapy may have inspired the reformation of another poor soul. Marilyn aided the comedy of her scene by lowering her tone and dropping the breathless quality of her voice to deliver unexpected lines as the sweet-faced streetwalker of O. Henry's story.

Act Three: The Platinum Years

*"I used to think as I looked at the Hollywood night,
`There must be thousands of girls sitting alone like me, dreaming of
becoming a movie star. But I'm not going to worry about them.
I'm dreaming the hardest."*

—MARILYN

Looking back the impression might be that Marilyn and stardom were meant to come together, that fate had to have made her way to becoming Hollywood's most famous star effortless. In the late '40s her face and figure may have been familiar from magazines and calendars, but she remained a nameless model. By the time the face met up with a name met up with a star showcase in a major film, six years had passed since her screen debut. Marilyn was young, at the peak of her beauty at age twenty-six, but it was not the rapid rise of, for instance, her idol, Jean Harlow (a star by age nineteen). When fame did come to Marilyn, it was with an intensity that was at times frightening, as it intruded on such private moments as her divorce from Joe DiMaggio or leaving the hospital after a miscarriage. And yet she thrived on the public's adoration.

Under the management of Johnny Hyde, young Marilyn had not taken on anything she wasn't ready for. She was seen in a handful of A productions and other small roles helped put her at ease before the cameras while gaining experience. Steadily she became Fox's number-one attraction. In *Gentlemen Prefer Blondes* and *The Seven Year Itch* she elevated the playing of a so-called dumb blonde to an art form. Unable to bear being thought of as a joke, however, she left for New York to study acting. Though she won major concessions from Fox, the relationship between Marilyn and her home studio was tenuous thereafter.

But following *O. Henry's Full House* in the spring of 1952, Marilyn was set to begin the first of her three hit films to release the following year. In the summer of 1962 she came full circle and returned to the Fox lot, where her final weeks were committed to film. In between those ten years, there was Marilyn, platinum in all her glory, a star then, a legend now.

Marilyn

"She's a tramp!
I'll tell you now so you won't have to ask."

••• Rose with Thorns

The most uncharacteristic character of Marilyn's years as a superstar, and the one that shot her into that realm in the first place, was Rose Loomis of *Niagara*. It was Marilyn's nineteenth film. The amoral Rose is an adulteress who plots to do away with her husband George during a vacation at Niagara Falls. George Loomis has been hooked on the beer hall waitress from Duluth since they met. Now unstable after action in the Korean War, it becomes as clear that Rose is necessary to his recovery as it is evident that she is bent on leading him to destruction.

Marilyn's camp performance was played opposite the experienced and respected Joseph Cotten, but it was unquestionably her show.

MARILYN AND JOSEPH COTTEN

The Look

Marilyn's "platinum" blonde hair was a more golden shade in Technicolor. Form-fitting skirts and blouses perhaps a size too small, high-heeled shoes with ankle straps, hoop earrings, lacquered lips, tousled hair—all signatures of Marilyn's Rose Loomis. She favors shades of red throughout, from her wardrobe to the high-gloss red lipstick that remains in place at all times, even in the shower.

COSTUME TEST FOR A SUIT DESIGNED BY DOROTHY JEAKINS.

SMUDGE-PROOF MAKEUP, UNDISTURBED BY WATER.

Marilyn and Whitey ————————————

Allan "Whitey" Snyder was key in establishing the look that would become instantly identifiable as "Marilyn." *Niagara* was one of their essential collaborations as he prepared the mesmerizing face he had made up for black and white film for its first great Technicolor showcase. Pre-Marilyn Snyder tended to the faces of Fox's top leading ladies: Betty Grable, Gene Tierney, Jeanne Crain, Linda Darnell, and Anne Baxter. He first beautified Marilyn for the color screen test that earned her a contract with Fox in 1946. Later he became her personal makeup artist. At Marilyn's side on the majority of her film sets, Snyder became her close confidante. Their partnership lasted from the start of Marilyn's career through to 1962, when he made her up once more for her funeral, and then served as pallbearer for his dear friend.

Honeymooners' Paradise?

An atmosphere of impending doom hangs over the famous falls as well as the Rainbow Cabins, where the brooding and possessive George Loomis (Joseph Cotten) wonders what his wife Rose is up to. Loomis is a war veteran recently discharged from an Army sanitarium. This is no rest cure, however, for Rose has taken as her lover the handsome Ted Patrick (Richard Allan). The couple plots to do away with Loomis, but their scheme backfires and Loomis murders Patrick instead. Rose is unaware that the tables have been turned.

Ray (Casey Adams) and Polly Cutler (Jean Peters), a young couple on their second honeymoon, find themselves hopelessly enmeshed in the intrigue—roped in by Rose, who at the outset seems to be genuinely concerned about the "disappearance" of her husband. Later, Loomis pleads for Polly's help to keep the police under the mistaken notion that he is dead—at least long enough for him to exact his revenge on his wife.

A menacing Loomis corners Rose in the deserted Carillon Tower and strangles her to death. Then the panicked killer again appeals to Polly for help in dodging the police. Although she refuses, his desperation eventually lands them on a perilous boat ride. Polly escapes just before Loomis perishes over the falls.

GEORGE IS SUSPICIOUS OF HIS BEAUTIFUL WIFE, WHO DOESN'T
DO ANYTHING TO RELIEVE HIS TORTURED MIND.

Polly Cutler spots Mrs. Loomis with another man.

Polly: "Didn't that Mrs. Loomis say she was going shopping?"

Ray: "Yeah. Why?"

Polly: "Well, she sure got herself an armful of groceries."

"Hey, get out the fire hose."

Ray Cutler intones the reaction of the resort guests to the sight of Rose. Much was made of Marilyn's beauty being played against the backdrop of Niagara Falls. Most felt that the falls came in a poor second.

"And parading around, showing herself off in that dress—cut down so low in front you can see her kneecaps!"

ROSE PLACES A CALL TO HER LOVER.

Casting Calls

Fox's choices, ordered by preference, as of February 15, 1952:

Rose Loomis: Marilyn Monroe, Anne Bancroft, Jean Peters, Lauren Bacall, Ava Gardner

George Loomis: Burt Lancaster, James Mason

Polly Cutler: Anne Francis, Anne Baxter, Anne Bancroft, Jeanne Crain

Ray Cutler: Dale Robertson

Other than Marilyn, none of director Henry Hathaway's leading cast members were mentioned yet. Casey Adams (better known in later years as Broadway performer Max Showalter) was ultimately cast as Ray, and to play his wife, Polly, former Miss Ohio State Jean Peters was selected. Peters was then a young contract actress at Fox, making $1,000 per week (to Marilyn's $500). She and Marilyn were the same age and both made their screen debuts at Fox in 1947. Peters made films for only two more years. Then in 1957 she married Howard Hughes.

DIRECTOR HENRY HATHAWAY CHATS WITH STARS MARILYN AND JOSEPH COTTEN.

On Location

One of the sites that could not be reproduced in a sound-stage or on the studio backlot was Niagara Falls. The cast and crew headed up to Ontario, Canada for location filming just after Marilyn's twenty-sixth birthday, in June 1952. She got to travel around much of the area and took a ride on the Maid of the Mist, the boat that ferries tourists to the falls.

A SET STILL OF THE INTERIOR OF THE NIAGARA FALLS CABIN SHARED BY GEORGE AND ROSE LOOMIS.

"Sure I'm meeting somebody. Just anybody handy—as long as he's a man.
How about the ticket seller himself? I could grab him on my way out.
Or one of the kids with the phonograph. Anybody suits me—take your pick."

A Word from the Censors...

The character of Rose Loomis and Marilyn's rendition of the part were startling in themselves. When the script of *Niagara* was submitted to the censorship board in the early months of 1952, many concerns were voiced, some of which were addressed by Fox, others not.

The censors wanted a new ending in which Loomis was properly punished for his crimes, instead of escaping sentence by what they felt was a suicide as the boat plummeted over the falls. In this battle, the original intent of the screenwriters was preserved.

Production Code Administration director Joseph I. Breen to Jason Joy at Fox:

"There should be no suggestion that Rose is sleeping
in the nude in scene 16."

SCENE 16 IN THE FINAL CUT:

Technicolor Film Noir

Despite its vivid color photography, *Niagara* has many elements to classify it in the shadowy world of film noir: the treacherous female lead, the score, noir veteran Joseph MacDonald's lighting and photography which exhibited sharp shadows and the genre's signature light streaming in through window blinds. The two-timing woman at the center of a sinister plot is classic film noir. Rose's devious machinations ultimately lead to ruin for her and the men fixated on her. Henry Hathaway had directed some of the foremost examples of film noir of the post–World War II period, including *The House on 92nd Street* and *Kiss of Death*.

CAREFUL LIGHTING AND CAMERA SETUPS COMPOSE THE LOOK OF *NIAGARA*.

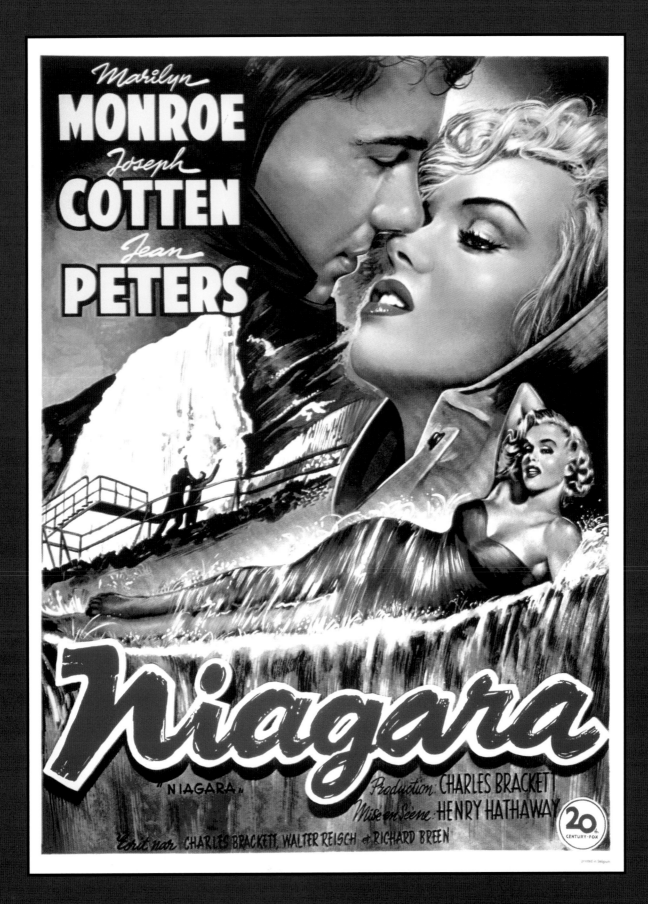

ROSE LISTENS TO HER FAVORITE SONG.

"There isn't any other song."

"Kiss"

Music by Lionel Newman, lyrics by Haven Gillespie. Marilyn, in a Technicolor glow, hummed a memorably sensuous interpretation of this song. The original plan was to use Cole Porter's "Night and Day" in the scene. A couple of lines of dialogue had to be modified because of the switch. George Loomis's outburst to Rose over " . . . that guy you think of day and night, night and day" became "this guy you sing to, hum to." Heard in everything from bells, whistles, saxophones, clarinets, to full orchestra arrangements, "Kiss" was the lovers' theme of *Niagara* and a ubiquitous background throughout the film.

Other song swaps: The piece heard before "Kiss," as Rose Loomis walks up to the boy running the phonograph to make her song request, was supposed to be "The Beer Barrel Polka." The "corny old tune" Rose says her husband would prefer to "Kiss" was originally "The End of a Perfect Day," instead of "In the Gloaming."

ROSE MAKES HER SONG REQUEST.

MARILYN LOOKS OVER HER SCRIPT WITH CO-STAR RICHARD ALLAN.

A Rude Awakening

Rose is taken to the morgue to identify what the police believe to be the remains of George Loomis. When she sees that the body belongs not to her husband but to her lover, Rose falls into a faint and must be taken to a hospital. The melody of "Kiss" played by the carillon bells has the power to penetrate through a deep state of sedation, bringing to consciousness the death of her lover and communicating the fact that her husband is alive and out for revenge.

From the final shooting script:

"On the bed, the still figure of Rose Loomis lies in a drugged peace . . . As the music becomes more and more recognizable, Rose begins to breathe more heavily. Sweat breaks out on the smooth forehead. Her hands clench. The lids of her eyes try to open, fight desperately against the opiate. . . . As the music hits the refrain, the eyelids win their struggle at last. They open heavily, drop, then rise again. The camera zooms up till only the two eyes fill the screen, and in those eyes is written mortal fear."

AT THE MORGUE, ROSE SEES NOT THE BODY OF HER HUSBAND BUT THAT OF HER LOVER.

The Carillon Tower Belfry

After murdering Rose, with a pained expression Loomis picks up her red lipstick encrusted with imitation jewels. As originally staged, he places it in Rose's lifeless hand saying, "Here's your lipstick. Wherever you are, you'll still be wanting it." He reaches out, gently touches her hair, and then speaks the line that remained in the film, "I loved you Rose. You know that."

"They can't play it for you now Rose."

CARILLON BELLS PLAYING HER SONG SIGNAL MESSAGES TO ROSE AT VARIOUS POINTS IN THE STORY.

Ray: "Why don't you ever get a dress like that?"

AT THE PARTY FOR THE UNVEILING OF RAY ANTHONY'S "MARILYN."

"Marilyn"

Soon there *was* another song associated with Marilyn in her *Niagara* period. Bandleader Ray Anthony wrote a song dedicated to her titled "Marilyn," and she wore the low-cut Dorothy Jeakins-designed dress of Rose Loomis at a party for her in August 1952, where the song was showcased. Marilyn also wore the "Rose" dress when she performed a guest spot on radio's Edgar Bergen-Charlie McCarthy program in November of that year.

Polly: "Listen. For a dress like that, you've got to start laying plans when you're about thirteen."

· Taglines ·

"Niagara and Marilyn Monroe—The Two Most Electrifying Sights in the World!"

"Marilyn as the tantalizing temptress . . . whose kisses fired men's souls."

"Niagara and Marilyn Monroe—the High Water Mark in Suspense."

Niagara was made on a budget of $1.25 million and earned $6 million in worldwide film rentals.
Public interest in Marilyn was at a fever pitch. It took considerable time for her home studio to admit it,
but the public had long since decided Marilyn was a star.

"You've been very kind but thanks, I'd rather WALK."

Marilyn's much-talked about manner of walking was displayed in one of the longest walks in cinema history. Indeed, the camera remains on her for many long walks in *Niagara*.

From here, she walked into the role that made her an icon . . .

···*The Blonde Gentlemen Prefer*

"Diamonds are a Girl's Best Friend," and in the case of Lorelei Lee, the feeling is entirely mutual. An eye-popping entertainer, loyal friend, and resourceful gold-digger, she can spot a millionaire a mile off. Her beauty attracts males as young as age ten, but it is her sweetness that captures the hearts of gentlemen like Gus Esmond and "Piggy," a slightly daft diamond mine owner who fairly reeks of precious gems. At times it may seem Lorelei was born yesterday, but she has some profound notions buzzing inside her platinum-topped head. Those who take her for dumb will be surprised. She has a perfect grasp on a great many essentials. Whether her aim at the moment is fixing seating arrangements to her inclination or sneaking incriminating photos from a peeping detective, she knows how to get what she wants. What she wants most is a millionaire, and with one as thoughtful as Gus in her life, she also knows it is just as easy to fall in love with a rich man as it is a poor one.

DUMB BLONDE? LORELEI CAN HANDLE ANY SITUATION, INCLUDING GETTING LOCKED IN A STATEROOM WITH A PORTHOLE AS THE ONLY ROUTE OF ESCAPE. ACCORDING TO LORELEI, SHE'S FOUND THAT MOST MEN DON'T LIKE A GIRL WITH SUCH BRAINS ——EXCEPT FOR GUS.

A Birthday Gift

In the 1920s, audiences enjoyed Anita Loos's story, *Gentlemen Prefer Blondes*, as a novel, a play, and a film. In late 1949, the musical comedy edition starring Carol Channing arrived on Broadway, where it was a smash hit for the next two years. Darryl Zanuck purchased the prized film rights for $500,000. Fox's leading blonde musical star, Betty Grable, might have seemed the obvious choice to star as Lorelei, but at this stage, casting Marilyn in the part was an intriguing alternative.

Unconvinced that she could handle the lead in a full-scale musical, Zanuck hesitated until he heard a sample of Marilyn's singing. Further tipping the scales in her favor, according to Fox records, Marilyn's salary continued to be $500 per week; therefore she would be a great deal less expensive than Grable, who received $150,000 per picture. On her twenty-sixth birthday, Marilyn received the news that she was to play the ultimate blonde, Lorelei Lee. Howard Hawks was slated to direct and Charles Lederer wrote the screenplay. Both had worked with Marilyn once before, on *Monkey Business*.

HAT'S OFF! MARILYN AS THE DARLING OF TWO CONTINENTS. LORELEI LEE

• Marilyn and Jane •

The 1928 film version of *Gentlemen Prefer Blondes* starred Ruth Taylor and Alice White. For the new edition, Fox borrowed raven-haired beauty Jane Russell from Howard Hughes—the man who discovered and held the actress under exclusive contract—to play the part of Dorothy Shaw. Marilyn and Russell contrasted and complimented one another beautifully both onscreen and off. They got along famously during filming and their comfort with each other is perceptible. They appear relaxed, confident, and unthreatened by the other's attributes. Marilyn was the blonde of the title and Russell was advertised as "The World's Most Talked-About Brunette."

Marilyn's inability to arrive to the set on time was already well-known by this time. Russell found the solution to the problem during the making of *Gentlemen Prefer Blondes* to be uncomplicated. She would simply stop for Marilyn on her way to the set, say "Come on, Blondie, it's time to go," and Marilyn would come along. In late 1952 at least, Marilyn just needed a bit of subtle encouragement to calm her intense nerves and keep the production on or close to schedule.

In 1955, Russell starred in a follow-up to *Gentlemen Prefer Blondes*, titled *Gentlemen Marry Brunettes*, which she made with Jeanne Crain.

The Road to Fortune

Lorelei Lee has found the man of her dreams—an agreeable and generous millionaire—in Gus Esmond (Tommy Noonan), but though he has slipped the diamond ring on her finger, they have not yet married because Gus's father forbids the union. Lorelei has a plan to take a trip to France, where Gus is sure to follow when he can no longer stand their separation. Lorelei soon heads for Europe on glamorous shipboard along with her best friend in the world, Dorothy Shaw.

Unlike Lorelei, Dorothy has no interest in money. Her weakness is for handsome types like Mr. Ernie Malone (Elliott Reid), whom she soon discovers is a detective hired by Gus's father to collect evidence against Lorelei. As this budding romance stops in its tracks, the benevolent owner of a diamond mine, Sir Francis Beekman (Charles Coburn)—better known as "Piggy"—becomes besotted by Lorelei. As a token of his affection, he presents her with his wife's diamond tiara, only to steal it from her in a less giving mood.

After the ship docks in France, Lorelei finds herself in trouble with the gendarmes as she is accused by Lady Beekman (Norma Varden) of having stolen the tiara. As a show of his love for Dorothy, Malone saves Lorelei by locating a truant Piggy in possession of the tiara. Reports of these activities immediately bring Gus and his father to France. Lorelei realizes she truly loves Gus and her charm soon convinces the elder Esmond. Gus's devotion to Lorelei is matched only by Malone's to Dorothy. At their double wedding, the brides' eyes sparkle like the diamonds on their hands.

LORELEI SHOWS OFF THE BAUBLE PRESENTED TO HER BY FIANCÉ GUS.

LADY BEEKMAN ENTRUSTS HER TIARA TO THE WORLD'S MOST FABULOUS DIAMOND
COLLECTOR FOR A FEW BRIEF MOMENTS.

LORELEI IS AS UNINTERESTED IN THE ATHLETES TRAVELING WITH HER TO EUROPE
AS THEY ARE FASCINATED BY HER.

Star on the Set

MARILYN REHEARSES A SCENE WITH JEAN DEL VAL, AS THE SHIP'S HEADWAITER, AND ELLIOTT REID (IN BACKGROUND).

Co-star Casting

For her romantic interest, Gus Esmond, Fox considered using Marilyn's past co-star, David Wayne; her future co-star Tom Ewell; Eddie Bracken; eventual selection Tommy Noonan; and Elliott Reid; who was instead signed for the part of Ernie Malone.

LORELEI MUST GET THE PRICE OF A TIARA OUT OF GUS. ANY CHANCE SHE'LL BE TURNED DOWN?

Kindred Souls?

Child actor George "Foghorn" Winslow was as identified with his distinctive voice as Marilyn was. His bass tones came out of the body of a six-year-old, even as Marilyn's aura of childlike innocence emanated from the body of a grown woman. They played a wonderful scene together after Lorelei sneaks into Malone's cabin and gets locked in. Lorelei must assure Mr. Spofford that she is not a "burgalar" so that he will assist in her escape through a porthole. Though not entirely convinced, he says he will help her for two reasons: 1) She has a lot of animal magnetism. 2) He's too young to be sent to jail.

MARILYN PREPARES TO FILM HER HILARIOUS SEQUENCE WITH GEORGE WINSLOW, THE YOUNG ACTOR WHO PLAYED HENRY SPOFFORD III.

Sugar and Spice

Partners onstage and best friends off, Lorelei and Dorothy are as devoted to each other as they come, in spite of their distinct personalities. Each girl worries that the other's taste in men will lead her to no good. While Lorelei dreams of millionaires, Dorothy is a self-confessed "hobo collector." Her ideal is a young man who can show her a good time—perhaps one of the many Olympic athletes who buzz around her between training exercises.

Convinced Dorothy will never be happy if she must worry about finances, a concerned Lorelei is set on finding her friend a moneyed companion. Trusting her passenger list, which omits details like a gentleman's age, Lorelei selects Mr. Henry Spofford III. Dorothy finds the six-year-old with an appreciation for beauty beyond his years amusing company, but she has someone older in mind.

LORELEI WITH HER FAVORITE DIAMOND MINE OWNER, PIGGY (CHARLES COBURN)

"The Two M-M-Marvels of our Age in the Wonder Musical of the World!" —*Fox publicity*

"The Best Friend a Diamond Ever Had"

So Marilyn was named by the Jewelry Academy in July 1953. The title would have more appropriately been given to Lorelei. A kiss on the hand is very nice, but diamonds are forever was the character's general feeling. Marilyn herself showed no particular interest in authentic jewels. For publicity photographs and public appearances she relied chiefly on the studio's collection.

(TOP) THE PUBLICITY DEPARTMENT HAD A FIELD DAY COMING UP WITH TAGLINES TO ATTACH TO ADVERTISEMENTS FEATURING MARILYN AND JANE RUSSELL.

DIAMONDS THAT GO ON YOUR HEAD? FINDING NEW PLACES TO WEAR DIAMONDS IS ONE OF FABULOUS LORELEI LEE'S GREATEST JOYS.

Marilyn and Travilla

Givenchy gave Audrey Hepburn a little black dress, Jean Louis made Rita Hayworth sizzle in *Gilda*, Adrian helped make Greta Garbo a goddess, and Marilyn had William Travilla to flatter her natural assets. Travilla was a Fox contract designer who worked under wardrobe director Charles Le Maire. He personally crafted the clothes worn by Marilyn both for industry functions and in the majority of her Fox films after she was elevated to star status. They had a friendly personal relationship, and unlike Garbo, who later told Adrian that she never liked the clothes he designed for her, Marilyn was delighted to be dressed by Travilla.

Marilyn-Travilla films:

Don't Bother to Knock
Monkey Business
Gentlemen Prefer Blondes
How to Marry a Millionaire
River of No Return
There's No Business Like Show Business
The Seven Year Itch
Bus Stop

LORELEI DISCUSSES HOW TO GET A POTENTIALLY INCRIMINATING ROLL OF FILM OUT OF THE POCKETS OF A SNEAKING DETECTIVE.

MARILYN WORE A WHITE VERSION OF HER MOST FAMOUS TRAVILLA-DESIGNED *BLONDES* GOWN TO AT LEAST THREE MAJOR HOLLYWOOD EVENTS IN 1953, INCLUDING THE PREMIERE OF *CALL ME MADAM*, PICTURED HERE.

Vocal Exercises

Marilyn's prior singing experience in films was limited. There had been two songs in *Ladies of the Chorus*, a low-budget musical made at Columbia Pictures in 1948, and the bit of humming she did of "Kiss" in *Niagara*. Much of the summer and early fall of 1952 Marilyn spent improving her singing by working with a coach before filming got under way on November 17, 1952. Marilyn participated in four production numbers in the picture. "Two Little Girls from Little Rock" and "When Love Goes Wrong" were sung by Marilyn and Jane Russell. Her solos were a verse of "Bye Bye Baby" and "Diamonds Are a Girl's Best Friend."

On September 13, 1953, Marilyn made her television debut on an episode of *The Jack Benny Show*, during which she sang "Bye Bye Baby" to the star.

THE "LITTLE ROCK" NUMBER HOOKS THE AUDIENCE, GETTING THE SHOW OFF TO A DAZZLING START.

"Four French Dances"

This third duet for Marilyn and Russell was filmed and then discarded. They are shown wearing the costumes once—the first time Gus goes backstage to talk to Lorelei after his arrival in France. A fleeting glimpse of the number itself, pictured above, is seen in the theatrical trailer.

THIS BRIEF SCENE DID MAKE THE FINAL CUT.

"Diamonds are a Girl's Best Friend"

When Marilyn delivered her electrifying rendition of the song by Jule Styne and Leo Robin, movie audiences discovered what they had been missing in the six-year wait for her to be cast in a large-scale musical. As it would be impossible to imagine a better musical role for her entrée into the genre, it was as though Marilyn and Fox had been waiting for *Gentlemen Prefer Blondes* to be ready for the screen again. Choreographed by Jack Cole, Marilyn performed with confidence and style that belied the fact that it was her first ever solo production number. With pink ballerinas flitting about and men falling at her feet, this often-imitated scene became Marilyn's signature musical routine and the song is inextricably linked with the star.

MARILYN AND THE MEN OF THE CHORUS REHEARSE THE CINEMA'S GREATEST TRIBUTE TO DIAMONDS.

An Alternate Dress

Travilla originally designed a revealing costume made up of little more than fishnet and rhinestones for "Diamonds Are a Girl's Best Friend," to be worn with a choker, tiara, black opera gloves, and a large black-feather fan-dancer's fan. The song glorifying authentic diamonds was to be performed by Marilyn draped in imitation jewels against a black backdrop. After costume tests were made they plainly lost their nerve. The costume was presumably not considered worth the certain controversy it would incite and Travilla was asked to cover Marilyn up. As a result, one of the two most famous gowns Marilyn ever wore was born—a perfect blend of class, flash, and whimsy that fitted her character and created in viewer's minds a memorable shock of pink against the deep-red background.

NEW YORK *HERALD TRIBUNE*: "MISS MONROE LOOKS AS THOUGH SHE WOULD GLOW IN THE DARK."

Shimmering Gold

Marilyn loved this pleated gold lamé halter-top gown designed by Travilla and wore it many times. The dress was passed from blonde to blonde beginning in early 1952, when Marilyn stopped by the set of *Dreamboat* and saw Ginger Rogers wearing it for a scene. Marilyn requested it from the wardrobe department. She wore it in publicity photos and wanted to wear it in *Gentlemen Prefer Blondes*, but it was deemed too revealing for the movies, so it can only be spotted briefly, from behind, as Lorelei dances the rumba with Piggy. Marilyn was sewn into it for the Photoplay Awards ceremony on March 9, 1953, when she was presented with a prize naming her the "Fastest Rising Star of 1952." It sparked considerable comment and disparaging remarks from Joan Crawford, which were made public in the syndicated column of Bob Thomas. Marilyn's supposed rival at Fox, Betty Grable, was one of few to defend Marilyn. She even wore the gown herself in 1954, during a *Shower of Stars* television special while performing "One for My Baby."

MARILYN DISPLAYS HER AWARD FROM *PHOTOPLAY* MAGAZINE "FOR HER RAPID RISE TO STARDOM IN 1952."

And the Winner Is . . .

Marilyn's progress and performances began to be recognized with awards:

• *Look*: Most Promising Female Newcomer of 1952

• Advertising Association of the West, February 1953: The Most Advertised Girl in the World

• *Photoplay*: Fastest Rising Star of 1952

• *Photoplay*: Best Actress, for her performances in *Gentlemen Prefer Blondes* and *How to Marry a Millionaire*

• *Redbook*, March 9, 1953: Best Young Box Office Personality

A Dream Come True

In Grauman's Chinese Theater ceremony number 104, Marilyn and Jane Russell left impressions of their signatures, hands, and high-heeled shoes in the theater's famed forecourt. The event took place on June 26, 1953, in connection with the release of *Gentlemen Prefer Blondes*, and attracted the largest crowd of spectators yet seen by the theater for the traditional ceremony. Marilyn's square was tinted yellow—or rather, blonde—and she dotted the "i" in "Marilyn" with a rhinestone that was promptly pried out by a fan. Both actresses recalled the many times as star-struck girls they attempted to fit their hands and shoes into the imprints of their movie idols. Footage of the event shows Marilyn and Russell both looking casually glamorous and on top of the world.

THE STAR EMERGES FROM HER DRESSING ROOM.

...The Marrying Kind...

With little break in between, Marilyn went from the gold-digging blonde Lorelei Lee to the gold-digging blonde Pola Debevoise in How to Marry a Millionaire, which began filming in April 1953. Nunnally Johnson, who had written her role of the beauty-contest queen in *We're Not Married*, wrote the screenplay, as well as produced the film, while the directorial reins went to Jean Negulesco. Johnson's story called for three beautiful actresses who could play comedy. Marilyn, Betty Grable, and Lauren Bacall fit these requirements, in addition to being popular box-office attractions. Johnson later said that he slanted the characters to the screen personas, if not the actual personalities, of the stars. Bacall would play Schatze, the sardonic brains of the girls' scheme; Grable would play the fun-loving Loco; and Marilyn the foggy blonde model, Pola.

Marilyn was not enthusiastic about playing the hopelessly near-sighted character, which would require her to wear glasses. She was partial to Grable's role of Loco, which in the script did read better than Pola. Ultimately, misted vision gave Marilyn many of the biggest laughs in the picture, and Pola's insecurity about her looks was an endearing distinction among Marilyn's characters.

"The way most people go about it, they use more brains picking a horse in the third at Belmont than they do picking a husband."

Setting a Bear Trap

Loco, Pola, and Schatze, fashion models and best friends, have merged their resources in the single-minded pursuit of millionaire husbands. Alas, even such enticing bait as raving beauty and a Sutton Place penthouse gets them nowhere until Loco finds them the "bear" to lead them to a herd of millionaires—cattle baron J. D. Hanley (William Powell). While Hanley is drawn to Schatze, Loco lures the rich (but married) Waldo Brewster (Fred Clark), and Pola links up with a phony oil tycoon, J. Stewart Merrill (Alex D'Arcy). Pola's nearsightedness saves her from Merrill when she boards a wrong plane and finds herself seated beside Freddie Denmark (David Wayne). Able to make her feel beautiful even behind glasses, he is the man for Pola. Loco, meanwhile, takes a trip to Maine where she hopes to find a fresh crop of rich men. She instead finds a handsome forest ranger (Rory Calhoun) who takes her back to New York—as his bride—just before Schatze is to be married to Hanley. Hanley loves Schatze, but knows she will be happier with her young suitor, Tom Brookman (Cameron Mitchell). Schatze believes Tom to be a poor "gas pump jockey," but must admit she loves him anyway. Having established that love is more important than money, the couples go out to celebrate and it is revealed that in Tom Brookman, Schatze actually has snagged a millionaire!

"Monroe, Grable, and Bacall, adding their own wonderful dimensions to the eye-filling dimensions of CinemaScope . . . letting you in on the grand and glorious adventures of three fascinating females who pool their beauty in the greatest plot against mankind since Helen of Troy, Marie Antoinette, and Venus DeMilo." –Fox publicity

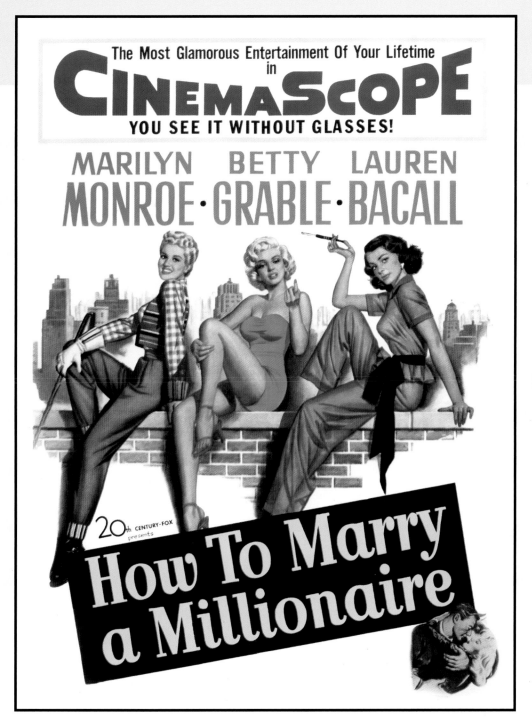

"The Big-Time, Grand-Time, Great-Time Show of All Time"

Introducing CinemaScope

Advertised as "The modern miracle you see *without* special glasses!" Fox pioneered this widescreen process as film studios scrambled with techniques like 3-D to compete with their rival moving into living rooms across the nation—television. With CinemaScope and new developments in stereophonic sound, Darryl Zanuck could state with confidence his studio's motto, "Movies are better than ever." *How to Marry a Millionaire* was the first picture to be filmed in CinemaScope, though its release was held until after *The Robe*, a high-drama biblical epic that would create a more spectacular showcase for the process.

Shot in an aspect ratio of 2.55:1 (in comparison to the previous standard of 1.33:1), *How to Marry a Millionaire* was a clever modern comedy that would show what CinemaScope could do for an entirely different kind of film from *The Robe*. It started with the Fox symphony orchestra performing "Street Scene," led by composer Alfred Newman, to entertain the audience while demonstrating the sweep of CinemaScope. The story then opened with newly filmed panoramic scenes of New York instead of the standard establishing shots of the city. Later on, the film's wide screen would show the ski-slopes of Maine, the models of a fashion show, and the lavish Manhattan apartment the girls share.

ONLY IN CINEMASCOPE—MOVIEGOERS HAD ZANUCK TO THANK FOR *FIVE* MARILYNS.

"The big question, `How does Marilyn Monroe look stretched across a broad screen?´ is easily answered. If you insisted on sitting in the front row, you would probably feel as though you were being smothered in baked Alaska." —*New York Herald-Tribune*

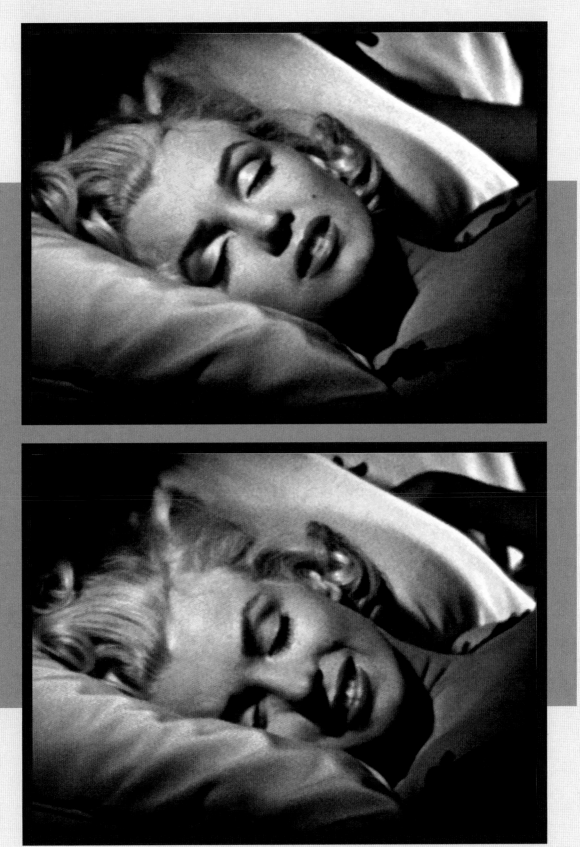

IN A MEMO TO JOHNSON AND NEGULESCO, ZANUCK POINTED TO THIS AS AN EXCEPTIONAL EXAMPLE OF HOW
TO FILM A CLOSE-UP IN THE NEW MEDIUM.

Hair and Makeup

PICTURE PERFECT AND READY
FOR HER CLOSE-UP.

TEST FOR THE CLOSE-UP ON POLA DREAMING.

Four Eyes

"Men seldom make passes at girls who wear glasses." No girl has taken more deeply to heart the Dorothy Parker couplet than Pola Debevoise. Consequently, the gorgeous but near-sighted Pola is plagued by insecurity and will not wear her specks before any male. This emotional handicap threatens to become physical as she regularly walks directly into walls, trips, runs into people, and holds books like *Murder by Strangulation* upside down while pretending to read. A trusting sort, she is apt to be taken in by a suave conman for a while, but the man who gives Pola confidence when her horn-rimmed spectacles are in place is naturally the one to win her heart. Freddie Denmark's near-blindness has gotten him into trouble too and they may have to take it on the lam for a time. Even so, with him, a happy vision for the future is clear.

"You know what they say about girls who wear glasses."

THE ONLY WAY TO TRAVEL . . .

Myopia Leads to Love

"Men aren't attentive to girls who wear glasses."

. . . Hence, no glasses—and a mistaken plane trip to Kansas City instead of Atlantic City, where the troubled Freddie is surprised to find one of the pretty girls who have leased his apartment.

WITH DAVID WAYNE

THE GLASSES GO ON FOR JUST A FEW SECONDS AS POLA CHECKS HER DRESS IN THE MIRROR BEFORE RETURNING TO HER DATE.

Freddie dares her to try her specks out on him.

Once they're on:

"You don't think they make me look like an old maid?"

"I've never seen anybody in my whole life that reminded me less of an old maid!"

POLA, CONFIDENT FREE OF GLASSES. WITH OR WITHOUT THEM, FREDDIE CONFIRMS SHE IS NO "OLD MAID" BY ANY STRETCH OF THE IMAGINATION.

Passing the Torch

As had just occurred with Jane Russell during the making of *Gentlemen Prefer Blondes*, Marilyn became friendly with a co-star who was expected to be her rival. Betty Grable was the pin-up queen of World War II with "Million Dollar Legs" (actually insured by Fox with Lloyds of London) and her saucy blonde persona in musicals made her the studio's number-one star for thirteen years. By 1953 she was slipping though, and Marilyn was the new sensation. Members of the press primed to report on a feud between the co-stars were disappointed. Off screen Grable was, according to Lauren Bacall, unpretentious and outgoing. Once, while the three actresses readied themselves to meet the press, Grable observed that Marilyn had neglected to paint her toenails. Knowing the waiting reporters would focus on Marilyn, she told her she could not see them like that, and began polishing Marilyn's toenails herself. Marilyn in turn had tremendous admiration for the top blonde of the '40s. Along with Jean Harlow, Grable was one of the actresses Marilyn studied intently and emulated during the years of her ascent to stardom.

Of her own accord, Grable walked out on her contract with Fox a short time after completing *How to Marry a Millionaire*, leaving her star dressing room on the Fox lot to Marilyn.

MARILYN WAS THE MAIN ATTRACTION FOR EVERY MANNER OF VISITOR TO THE SET—ABOVE, SEEN OUTSIDE BETTY GRABLE'S DRESSING ROOM.

IN THIS SCENE, POLA AND LOCO ACT AS BRIDESMAIDS AT SCHATZE'S WEDDING.

JEAN NEGULESCO CHATS WITH MARILYN AND BETTY GRABLE ON THE SET, GRATEFUL NOT TO HAVE TO PLAY MEDIATOR BETWEEN THE TWO SUPPOSED "BATTLING BLONDES" (AS SOME EARLY REPORTS INTIMATED IN HOPES ON DRUMMING UP A FEUD).

Marilyn and Grable were there for each other away from the set as well. With Joe DiMaggio and Harry James (Grable's bandleader husband) both out of town, Marilyn and Grable acted as each other's escorts to Walter Winchell's star-studded fifty-sixth birthday party on May 13, 1953. Marilyn attended wearing a white version of her pink "Diamonds Are a Girl's Best Friend" gown.

GRABLE ON MARILYN:
"She did an awful lot to boost things up for movies, when everything was at a low state; there'll never be anyone like her for looks, for attitude, for all of it."

Schatze

Lauren Bacall, the siren of *To Have and Have Not* and *The Big Sleep*, was an unlikely choice to accompany Marilyn and Betty Grable in *How to Marry a Millionaire* in that she had never before played in comedy. She had recently come under contract to Fox and expressed interest in this project to Zanuck. She submitted to a screen test that confirmed her ability to play the sharp-witted Schatze.

Both of Marilyn's co-stars were already well-established in Hollywood and they knew the publicity campaign was centered on Marilyn. Rather than inspiring competitiveness, the onslaught of the press made Bacall and Grable feel protective of her. The vulnerability she projected brought this quality out in both the women and men in Marilyn's life.

Definitely the biting comic of the trio, Schatze loves her bubble-headed roommates, but she can't resist taking occasional jabs at them. This exchange between Schatze and Tom Brookman was discarded from the script:

Tom asks if her friends have written to her. Schatze responds that it is impossible:

FRENCH (AND DUTCH) POSTER FOR *HOW TO MARRY A MILLIONAIRE* SHOWING THE THREE HAPPY CO-STARS.

"Pola writes with the wrong end of the pen and Loke needs help to stick the stamp in the right corner."

Girl Talk

Pola: "You know who I'd like to marry?"

Loco: "Who?"

Pola: "Rockefeller."

Loco: "Which one?"

Pola: "I don't care."

Loco: "I wouldn't mind marrying a Vanderbilt."

Pola: "Or Mr. Cadillac."

Schatze: "No such person. I checked."

Pola: "Did you see this fellow I'm with?"

Loco: "I saw him."

Pola: "What's he look like?"

Loco: "Very nice for a one-eyed man."

Pola: "Is that all he's got?"

Schatze: "Well, what do you think he's got that patch on for?"

Pola: "I didn't know it was a patch. I thought somebody might have belted him!"

HOT DOGS. CHAMPAGNE. BEST FRIENDS TO TALK UP FUTURE PLANS WITH ON A ROOFTOP TERRACE. "PEOPLE THAT LIVE ANY OTHER WAY ARE JUST CRAZY."

DISREGARDING THE EYE PATCH, SCHATZE'S ADVICE, AND EVEN THE FACT THAT HIS LAST NAME ISN'T CADILLAC, POLA'S ECSTATIC TO HEAR FROM THE MYSTERIOUS MR. MERRILL (AKA "BLINKY").

A Fox Favorite

One of Fox's favorite storylines, *How to Marry a Millionaire* was one of many films that were based on, or borrowed elements from, the Zoe Akins play *The Greeks Had a Word for It*. Samuel Goldwyn produced the first screen adaptation in 1932 under the title of *The Greeks Had a Word for Them*. After that, Fox produced *Three Blind Mice*, *Moon Over Miami* (which also starred Betty Grable), *Three Little Girls in Blue*, then the version starring Marilyn, and finally a television series titled *How to Marry a Millionaire* that premiered in 1957 and starred Barbara Eden. 1953's *How to Marry a Millionaire* was also based on the play *Loco* by Dale Eunson and Katharine Albert.

LAST MINUTE TOUCHES BEFORE FILMING ONE OF HER FIRST SCENES.

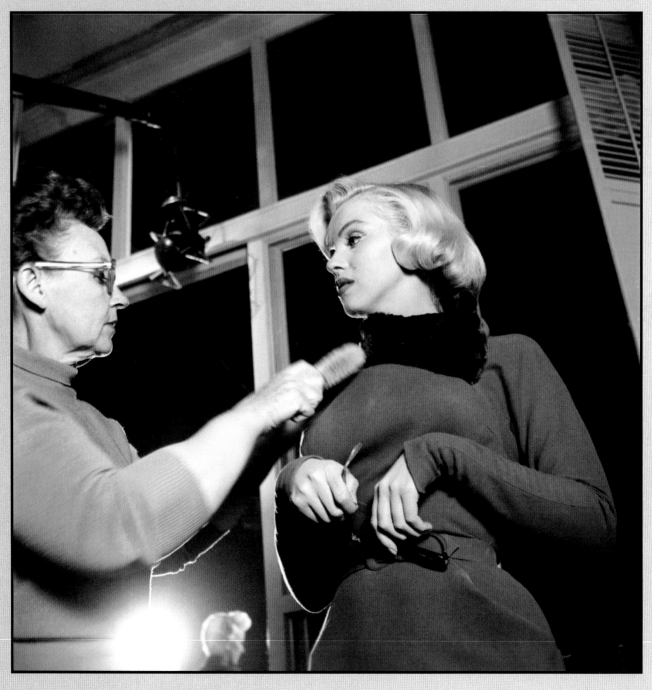

Casting Calls

In late November 1952, shortly after Marilyn began filming *Gentlemen Prefer Blondes* and before Nunnally Johnson had written his script, Fox had other casting ideas for *The Greeks Had a Word for It* (working title of *How to Marry a Millionaire*):

Schatze Page: Lauren Bacall, Jane Wyman, Anne Baxter

Loco Dempsey: Marilyn Monroe, Jane Russell, Lizabeth Scott, Shelley Winters

Pola Debevoise: Gloria DeHaven, Gloria Grahame, Jean Arthur, Jean Peters, Veronica Lake, Ann Sothern, Ann Sheridan

THE GIRLS HOPE FOR THE BEST FOR EACH OTHER. POLA IS ELATED TO OVERHEAR TALK OF MARRIAGE BETWEEN SCHATZE AND MILLIONAIRE J.D. HANLEY.

By the time Marilyn was cast in this film her salary had finally broken the $500 per week mark, though she was still making far less than her worth to Fox merited. She now earned $750 per week, the same amount paid for the services of co-star Alex D'Arcy, whose role was fairly small.

WITH CO-STAR ALEX D'ARCY AND ZANUCK'S MISTRESS, ACTRESS BELLA DARVI.

A Word from the Censors...

No arduous battles were fought against the censorship board over *How to Marry a Millionaire*. After Joseph Breen of the Production Code Administration reported that the script was acceptable, general admonitions were put forth, including ensuring the costumes of the ladies not be revealing.

The censors also requested that a flashback scene set in a divorce court be cut from the script. This was an omission from the scene in which Schatze tells Pola and Loco about her former husband. Her attitude toward marriage was considered to be too flippant.

SWIMSUITS WERE A CONCERN OF THE CENSORS, THOUGH MARILYN'S BEJEWELED COSTUME WAS NOT PROBLEMATIC.

"You know of course that DIAMONDS ARE A GIRL'S BEST FRIEND. And this, is our proof of it."

Double Frozen Daiquiris

In the fashion show sequence it was initially intended for Marilyn to model the "Double Frozen Daiquiris" beach costume, but a certain sizzling musical performance that everyone was talking about inspired a change of plans. The original staging of the fashion show had Marilyn enter wearing the jacket seen in the photos below. This was changed at the censors' request to have it established from the first moment that she was indeed wearing something underneath. The jacket was changed to the one seen in the color photo above, which was opened in front, keeping the swimsuit visible.

A Model Mannequin

William Travilla's designs for the three leading ladies earned him an Academy Award nomination, though the prize that year went to none other than *The Robe*.

POLA OPENS THE FASHION SHOW STAGED FOR MR. BROOKMAN.

Costume Testing

TEST FOR A COSTUME ON RIGHT NOT USED IN THE FINAL
FILM. ABOVE COSTUME WAS USED.

"What happened to all those rich millionaires everybody was talking about?"

First in Line

In the official credits of *How to Marry a Millionaire*, Betty Grable received top billing, but because she had departed from the studio prior to the film's release, Marilyn's name was promoted to first place in advertisements. All eyes were on Marilyn in the film in 1953 even as they are over half a century later due to her mythic status. Some fans of the film have their favorite, but none of the stars actually "stole the show" from the other two. Each of the actresses was at her comic best.

How to Marry a Millionaire had its lavish premiere on November 4, 1953. The picture was a great success at the box office, earning $7.3 million in film rentals.

"The Indians call it the RIVER OF NO RETURN.
From here on you'll find out why."

Marilyn Monroe: Platinum Fox – River of No Return

DOWN THE RIVER TO COUNCIL CITY

••• Marilyn in Canada

Location shooting for *River of No Return* sent Marilyn to the national parks of Alberta, Canada in August 1953. The crew took full advantage of the picturesque locale with the wide lenses of CinemaScope, but the general consensus was that ravishing Marilyn was equal to the competition.

MARILYN RELAXES AS BEST SHE CAN WITH EVER-PRESENT PHOTOGRAPHERS
ON LOCATION IN CANADA IN 1953.

In the Name of Art

This was a difficult shoot for Marilyn. There was tension between her and director Otto Preminger, mostly as a result of Marilyn's great reliance on her drama coach, Natasha Lytess, which infuriated Preminger. The filming was also physically taxing. The director insisted that his stars perform the scenes going down the rapids themselves, without benefit of stunt doubles. When the raft became unmanageable on the river, Marilyn and Mitchum had to be rescued. Another such incident made headlines. After falling from the raft into the cold Athabasca River, Marilyn injured her left ankle and walked on crutches for a few days, though it was suspected the crutches served more as props to soften Preminger's attitude toward her. Shortly after the accident, Joe DiMaggio cheered up the production for Marilyn by joining her in Canada for the final two weeks of filming.

A Raging River

As gold rush fever rages in the untamed Northwest, Matt Calder (Robert Mitchum), a homesteader recently released from prison, reunites with his son, Mark (Tommy Rettig), whose mother has died. The one friend of nine-year-old Mark is Kay (Marilyn), a saloon singer and fiancée of crooked gambler Harry Weston (Rory Calhoun). Weston has "won" a gold claim which he must file in Council City in a hurry—before the man he cheated catches up with him. Not owning a horse of his own, Weston steals Matt's only horse and rifle to make the trip to Council City by land. Kay stays behind.

Weston's theft leaves Kay, Matt, and Mark defenseless against an attack by warring Indians. Their only means of escape is a raft to ride the treacherous waters. Along the way to Council City, where both Matt and Kay are anxious to meet up with Weston, Matt, Kay, and Mark battle each other, Indians, and a river aptly nicknamed the "River of No Return." Facing these ordeals together creates a close bond between them by the time they reach Council City. Matt and Kay share an unspoken love for one another, although her plan to marry Weston has not changed.

Knowing Matt is going after him for revenge, Kay pleads with Weston to explain to Matt why he stole the horse and rifle. She believes it was an act of desperation, but soon she realizes Weston is plain ruthless. When he and Matt meet up, Weston attempts to kill Matt. Mark saves his father's life with a rifle fired at Weston. Father and son set out to rebuild their farm. They have a fine chance for happiness—Kay is going with them.

WITH RORY CALHOUN, KAY DISCOVERS THE TRUE CHARACTER OF THE MAN SHE PLANNED TO MARRY.

A WORN OUT KAY MUST ENDURE A FINAL SHOWDOWN IN COUNCIL CITY.

KAY IS A VISION IN THE SPOTLIGHT OF A SALOON WHERE THE WORDS SHE SINGS MOVE HER TO TEARS AND THE PATRONS TO SILENCE.

THE TRUE MARK OF A PROFESSIONAL GLAMOUR STAR—ABLE TO LOOK POSITIVELY CHEERFUL
THROUGH THE CONFINES OF A CORSET.

Marilyn in a Western?

It was late 1953 and Marilyn the screen goddess was at her peak. Coming off of *Gentlemen Prefer Blondes* and *How to Marry a Millionaire*, for *River of No Return* to be next in line for Marilyn seemed incongruous. She may have welcomed a change from "dumb blonde" types, but this was not what she had in mind, later saying she felt the actors were of secondary importance, after the scenery. Still, the part was not all bad for Marilyn, and she made the most of its good points. It was a dramatic role that did not require the actress who brought it to life to be the sex goddess of the nation. She did not play it as another Lorelei Lee. Her voice was keyed lower and the breathiness was omitted. Marilyn also had her first strong leading man in Robert Mitchum. Like Betty Grable before her, with such a potent box office personality, it was not considered necessary to pair either star with a major male lead, so the opportunities for them to appear with actors on par with Spencer Tracy, James Stewart, and the like were all but nonexistent.

MARILYN WITHSTOOD THE UNCOMFORTABLE CORSET OF HER PERIOD COSTUME TO ACHIEVE THE REQUISITE CINCHED WAIST FOR THE DRESSES SHE WORE IN THE FILM.

A BIT OF HOSING DOWN MAINTAINED A FRESH-FROM-THE-RIVER LOOK FOR THE ACTORS.

The Saloon Songstress

The pale blonde torch singer's light is unreal in the prospector's outpost of Tent City. Kay has evidently taken a lot of hard knocks, but among children, or when treated with respect, she exposes a heart aching for a setting in which she can drop her guard. Not having the best judgment, Kay places her trust in an unscrupulous crook like Weston. Her kind nature does not allow her to leave Matt and Mark when Matt is badly injured by Weston, and she is nothing if not game when facing the wilderness with a little boy and a forceful man who has a low opinion of her. When she does wrong, like revealing that Matt's absence from Mark's life was caused by Matt's being sent to prison, she is quick to make amends. All along, Kay hangs on to a pair of once-elegant high-heeled shoes to which she attaches some fond memory of better times, but at their journey's end she gladly lets them go for Matt, certain the best of times are yet to come.

"You get somebody in trouble, you get right in it with 'em."

MARILYN AND TOMMY RETTIG, LEERY OF EACH OTHER BRIEFLY IN THE FILM——AND OFF SCREEN, TOO, FOR A TIME.

"Down in the Meadow"

ONE OF KAY'S FAVORITE SONGS, AS IT REMINDS HER OF LIFE BEFORE SHE CAME TO THE GOLD CAMP.

"River of No Return"

THE SONG WAS PERFORMED BY TENNESSEE ERNIE FORD IN VOICEOVER AT THE OPENING AND CLOSE OF THE FILM, AS WELL AS BY MARILYN IN A MELANCHOLY MOOD AFTER PARTING WAYS WITH MATT AND MARK.

Marilyn and Mitchum

Marilyn met Robert Mitchum years before she ever stepped before a movie camera, even before she became a model. She was Norma Jeane Dougherty then, and Mitchum was an employee at the Lockheed aircraft factory with her then-husband, James Dougherty. *River of No Return* was the only picture Marilyn and Mitchum made together. No one, including the two stars, considered it a great film in their careers. With a project they were more fond of and under better filming circumstances, they might have been dynamite together.

> "Some other time in some other place, we might have even gotten along."

"This one and I are old friends."

"She's beautiful, isn't she?"

Girl and Boy

Marilyn, whose great desire in later years was to become a mother, adored children. The feeling was generally mutual, except in the case of Tommy Rettig during the first few days of production. Marilyn was stung by his coldness and had a talk with him about it, during which it was revealed that his priest had advised against socializing with the Number-One Sex Symbol. The ice broken, thereafter Marilyn and Rettig's friendship grew and she was his date at the premiere of his film, *The 5,000 Fingers of Dr. T.*

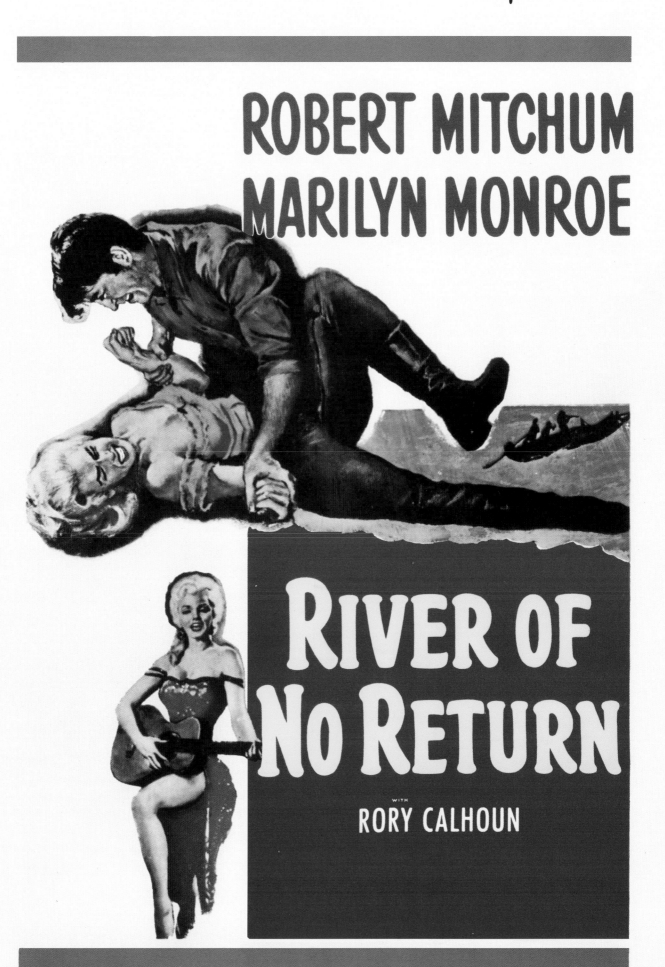

Going Once . . .

One of the first to show the attractiveness of blue jeans on the screen, Marilyn wore the then-strictly casual attire throughout the better part of three films, *River of No Return*, *Clash by Night*, and *The Misfits*. The three pairs she wore in *River of No Return* were among a great many of Marilyn's personal items sold to the highest bidder at Christie's Auction House in 1999. This lot went to designer Tommy Hilfiger for $42,550.

The lace-trimmed cotton pantaloons Marilyn wore in *River of No Return* were put on the auction block at Bonham's and Butterfields in November 2006 and sold for £4,100.

A COSTUME TEST MADE OF MARILYN IN THE BLUE JEANS WON BY TOMMY HILFIGER AT AUCTION IN 1999.

MARILYN ALL AGLOW BETWEEN TAKES, WEARING HER LACE-TRIMMED PANTALOONS.

The Girl in Pink Tights

Although it was not a blockbuster, *River of No Return* certainly did not harm Marilyn's status, but she was not happy. Her own assignment of choice after *How to Marry a Millionaire* had been that of the deadly seductive Nefer in Fox's production of *The Egyptian*, but Zanuck instead gave the part to his new protégé, Bella Darvi, and placed Marilyn in *River of No Return*. Next slated for her was *The Girl in Pink Tights*, a remake of the 1943 Betty Grable musical *Coney Island*. Even though Frank Sinatra was promised as her co-star, Marilyn refused the picture. As a contract actress, Marilyn was expected to take whatever film she was assigned. Her request to read the script had at first been denied, and when it was later delivered to Marilyn, her doubts about the project were confirmed. Failing to report to work on the scheduled first day of filming, she was placed on suspension in January 1954 and Fox announced that a newcomer, twenty-three-year-old Sheree North, would replace Marilyn in the film (and hinted that North would be assigned any other projects Marilyn might give them trouble about in the future). It was only a ploy to get Marilyn to acquiesce. *The Girl in Pink Tights* was cancelled and her suspension was lifted.

ON LOCATION, MARILYN DRIES HER WARDROBE ON THE ROCKS.

Marilyn DiMaggio

In the midst of the disputes between Marilyn and Fox about whether or not she would make *The Girl in Pink Tights*, Marilyn married her boyfriend of two years, Joe DiMaggio. She spent the New Year holiday in San Francisco with the DiMaggio family, and then on January 14, 1954, Marilyn and DiMaggio were married in a civil ceremony held at the San Francisco City Hall.

MARILYN AND JOE

AT A PRESS CONFERENCE SOON AFTER HER ARRIVAL IN JAPAN.

Pin-up on the Front

The newlyweds traveled to Japan on a tour for DiMaggio in February 1954. Shortly after their arrival in Tokyo, Marilyn was requested to make a side trip to entertain the U.S. troops stationed in Korea. She immediately accepted the invitation. Met by tens of thousands of grateful soldiers, she later called the experience the "highlight" of her career.

··· Back in Business ·

After shooting movies almost back to back for four years, when principal photography began on *There's No Business Like Show Business* on May 29, 1954, Marilyn had not worked on a film for over six months. Certainly not out of the spotlight, her myriad activities in that period—challenging the studio, marrying a baseball hero, traveling to Japan and Korea, attending industry events, and then living quietly for some weeks with Joe DiMaggio and family in San Francisco—were well-covered in the press.

Accepting that she would not make *The Girl in Pink Tights*, the studio was anxious to get Marilyn back before the cameras. That spring Zanuck toyed with the idea of asking her to play the title role in *The Queen of Sheba*, but the project never got off the ground. During the summer of 1954, Marilyn's contract was being renegotiated between Fox and her new agent, Hugh French, of Charles K. Feldman's Famous Artists Agency. Marilyn wanted a measure of creative input on her projects—and a much deserved salary increase. It was agreed that she would play the plum leading role in *The Seven Year Itch*, and in the meantime she would add her magnetic presence to *There's No Business Like Show Business*, a film already cast with a number of talented performers but no surefire box office names.

COSTUME TESTS OF MARILYN IN THE ROLE OF VICKY.

Screenwriters Phoebe and Henry Ephron (who took over for Lamar Trotti after his death in August 1952), wrote the character of Vicky into the script only after Marilyn was set to appear in the film. The difficulty came in expanding the part as much as possible for her. Marilyn, as usual, worked hard, giving it her all as she was placed in the company of seasoned musical performers Ethel Merman, Dan Dailey, Donald O'Connor, Mitzi Gaynor, and Johnnie Ray. Breezy and energetic, with boyish looks (though one year older than Marilyn), O'Connor was her romantic interest. He was the juvenile type and Marilyn's Vicky was no ingénue.

Not having the extensive musical background of her co-stars made Marilyn nervous. From the vast difference in styles on display, it is evident two choreographers were responsible for the film's production numbers. While Robert Alton staged the majority of the routines, Marilyn was permitted her choreographer of choice, Jack Cole, with whom she had worked on *Gentlemen Prefer Blondes* and *River of No Return*. Most of the *Show Business* numbers were marked by boundless energy, but not Marilyn's. A clear case in point is "Lazy." As Marilyn languishes on a couch, O'Connor and Mitzi Gaynor cavort tirelessly around her. Marilyn later said she was disappointed with her numbers.

THE DONAHUES (ETHEL MERMAN, DAN DAILEY, MITZI GAYNOR, AND DONALD O'CONNOR), GREET THE GIRL WHO JUST "STOLE" THE "HEAT WAVE" NUMBER FROM THEM—WHILE STILL WEARING THE COSTUMES THEY INTENDED TO WEAR FOR THE PERFORMANCE.

"That girl who steals everybody's material..."

This bit of art imitated life. As the screenwriters labored to stretch Marilyn's role of Vicky,

it was necessary to give her songs intended for other cast members.

Getting What She Wants

Vicky's performance of "After You Get What You
Want You Don't Want It" starts her off on her career
by impressing an important Broadway producer.

Turning up the HEAT

Marilyn, a sexy dance, costume, and musical arrangement of "Heat Wave," all conspired to produce a scandalous film sequence in 1954.

MARILYN AND CHORUS BOYS PERFORM THE SAMBA-INFUSED "HEAT WAVE" NUMBER.

Taking it Easy

MARILYN PERFORMS "LAZY" WITH DONALD O'CONNOR AND MITZI GAYNOR.

The Reason She Was "Lazy"?

. . . Maybe she just did not feel well. The purpose of Marilyn's visit to Korea had been to please the soldiers. Her dress for performances would help accomplish her objective whether or not it was appropriate for sub-zero temperatures. As a result, Marilyn came down with a bronchial infection that was still affecting her during the making of *There's No Business Like Show Business*. Marilyn had throat problems and even fainting spells on the set, prompting speculation that the newlywed Mrs. DiMaggio was pregnant. Alas, she was not.

"What a Family!"

By the early 1920s, Terry (Dan Dailey) and Molly (Ethel Merman), the popular vaudeville pair known as The Two Donahues, have three children. Born with show business in their hearts, years later Katie (Mitzi Gaynor), Tim (Donald O'Connor), and Steve (Johnnie Ray) change the billing to The Five Donahues by joining the act, making them the first family of the stage. Katie prefers dancing; Steve is a singer— until he shocks the family by quitting show business to join the priesthood.

Tim, the youngest, is a rascal with an eye for the ladies. He falls hard for Vicky (Marilyn), a rising performer of abundant ambition. When she gets her first starring role on Broadway she asks Tim and Katie to join her. They accept, leaving only two Donahues in the family act once more. While with Vicky's show, Tim becomes convinced that Vicky is having a romance with their producer. He goes on a drinking binge and is responsible for an auto accident in which he hurts himself and one of the show's chorus girls. Ashamed of himself, Tim disappears. The family searches in vain for nearly a year—a year in which Vicky realizes how much she loves Tim.

Molly blames Tim's disappearance on Vicky, with whom Katie tricks Molly into sharing a dressing room on the night of an Actors' Fund Benefit. It is then that Vicky manages to convince Molly of her love for Tim. This is also the night Tim returns, having been away with the Navy. He knows he was wrong about Vicky and is ready to take to the stage again. Steve—now Father Donahue—is also on hand. The Five Donahues (plus Vicky!) are reunited on stage for a rendition of "There's No Business Like Show Business."

TIM PRETENDS TO BE A REPORTER TO GET NEAR VICKY.

MARILYN LISTENS IN ON A JOKE AS MITZI GAYNOR AND ETHEL MERMAN KEEP THEIR TRAVILLA GOWNS
WRINKLE-FREE BETWEEN SCENES BY RESTING AGAINST BOARDS.

Styling the Stars

The extensive cast wardrobe by William Travilla and Miles White was nominated for an Academy Award. Marilyn was given some of her most risqué onscreen ensembles. There were high slits, an abbreviated hat-check girl uniform, a gown of flesh-colored stocking under white and silver sequins, a samba skirt which opened wide in the front, revealing a brief, two-piece black costume. There were also elegant items in her wardrobe, among them a white and rose dress and a beige suit. Curiously, most of the fashions are more distinctly mid-1950s than late '30s/early '40s, when most of the story takes place.

The Hat-check Girl

When first they meet, Tim thinks only of Vicky, but Miss Victoria Hoffman thinks only of becoming a star. Hoping to become an actress as well as a singer and dancer, this ambitious checkroom girl studies Chekhov and takes elocution lessons to the extreme. Under the tutelage of a sharp producer who shows the offending vocal coach the door, an entire revue, *Manhattan Parade*, is built around Vicky in record time. Also given a new name, "Vicky Parker" is a heartbreaker. As Tim

tries to pin down his career-minded dream girl, it is easy for him to jump to the wrong conclusion about Vicky's relationship with her producer. Only much later is she given the chance to let him know that Cupid's arrow has struck her, too. Still, a girl like Vicky has no intention of quitting show business for the traditional role of house-wife. Fortunately, given his history, Tim would not ask her to. It is more likely the next Molly and Terry Donahue are on their way to greatness.

"Check your hat, Sirrr?"

ALL SMILES AND SPARKLE AS STAR VICKY PARKER

ON THE SET MARILYN SHOWS JUST HOW SHORT
A HAT-CHECK GIRL'S UNIFORM CAN BE.

"A Man Chases a Girl (Until She Catches Him)"

Though they don't have any duets in the film, this publicity still portrays Marilyn and O'Connor as the Dancing Donahues.

The above title was Donald O'Connor's big number in the film. It follows Tim and Vicky's first date and is performed by O'Connor solo as the haunting voice of the hard-to-get Marilyn echoes from time to time.

Orchids to Irving

As much—if not more—a salute to the songwriter as it was a nod to show business in general, *There's No Business Like Show Business* was only one among many films that showcased the songs of Irving Berlin. Thin on plot, but fun to watch, films such as *Top Hat*, *Alexander's Ragtime Band*, *Holiday Inn*, *Blue Skies*, *Easter Parade*, *Annie Get Your Gun*, and *White Christmas*, featured a multitude of Berlin tunes. Marilyn would meet the composer later that year at a party in New York.

THE BIG FINALE. "THERE'S NO BUSINESS LIKE SHOW BUSINESS" PERFORMED BY MARILYN WITH STARS JOHNNIE RAY, MITZI GAYNOR, DAN DAILEY, ETHEL MERMAN, AND DONALD O'CONNOR.

"Hey! I just washed my hair!"

Six words spoken from the window of a New York City brownstone apartment at 164 East 61st Street that tied up a city block for four hours by drawing hundreds of spectators. This was only the beginning. It was September 1954, and Marilyn, director Billy Wilder, and company, were in town to film scenes for *The Seven Year Itch*. Every move they made was capitalized upon by Fox publicists and the press.

> "The sporadic infidelity pattern...
> in the middle-aged husband rises sharply
> during the seventh year of marriage."

NEXT TIME RICHARD WILL TAKE DR. BRUBAKER'S ADVICE AND NEVER TRY TO
COMMIT AN ACT OF TERROR PRECARIOUSLY BALANCED ON A PIANO BENCH.

Wishful Thinking

Marilyn's prize at the end of filming *There's No Business Like Show Business* in August of 1954 was stepping into a role known

simply as "The Girl," in *The Seven Year Itch*. With a screenplay by Billy Wilder and George Axelrod, the film was, as Marilyn

suspected it would be, her best comedy at Fox. Based on Axelrod's hit play, the story was about Richard Sherman, a middle-

aged New York husband whose wife and son escape to the comfort of Maine for the summer, leaving him behind to his job

in the steaming city, and his even more sizzling upstairs neighbor. One look at The Girl gives the seven-years-married man

the *itch*, sending his fevered imagination into overdrive. Their friendly encounters soon turn into an affair in his mind. He

dreads the lurid "details" may reach his wife at any minute, sending her down on him with a loaded revolver (because she'll

never believe he spent the entire night wrapping a paddle!).

"When it's hot like this, you know what I do?
I keep my undies in the icebox."

910-X-46

A COCKTAIL SHAKER, A TOMATO PLANT, AND AN ICEBOX—UNLIKELY ITEMS THAT SPARK CONVERSATION BETWEEN RICHARD AND THE GIRL IN THIS
SCENE, LEADING TO THE START OF THEIR SUMMER "ROMANCE."

The Seven Year Itch
vs. the Censors

George Axelrod's play opened on Broadway in 1952. He had written the story of a man who has an affair while his wife is away for the summer. The Hays Office warned Fox that a film based on *The Seven Year Itch* would violate the production code, which stated that adultery "must not be the subject of comedy or farce or treated as the material for laughter." What could be done on the New York stage was considered too hot for the film, which would reach a wider audience, playing in all parts of the country.

Director Billy Wilder was an old hand at sidestepping the code with daring films like *Double Indemnity* and *The Lost Weekend*. In the film version of *The Seven Year Itch*, the affair takes place entirely in Richard Sherman's mind. Wilder and Axelrod feared that the required changes would cause the original story to lose its appeal. With Marilyn on board there was no chance of that. What risqué material was lost from the play was more than made up for by her presence. In fact, Marilyn's hypnotic appeal stole the show in what was essentially the man's story.

A CENSORSHIP CUT: A PLUMBER, PLAYED BY VICTOR MOORE, WHO SUCCESSFULLY FREES THE GIRL'S TOE FROM HER BATHTUB FAUCET DROPS HIS WRENCH IN THE WATER AND FUMBLES FOR IT AS SHE IS STILL IN THE TUB.

Becoming The Girl

TRAVILLA-DESIGNED COSTUME TEST

HAIR AND MAKEUP TEST

"You may not believe this, but people keep falling desperately in love with me . . ."

"Remember me? The Tomato from Upstairs."

The Girl is a sweet-natured actress whose smile brightens the *Dazzledent Toothpaste Hour* every other week. Also a model, her picture has received honorable mention in *U.S. Camera*. In between time, she dodges impulsive proposals of marriage. Unaware of her affect on members of the opposite sex, she knows how to make even a homely man like Richard Sherman feel like Don Juan. A Denver native, she can't stand the heat of her first New York summer anymore than her new friend can, but she has a handful of tricks to stay cool, including catching the updraft from an occasional subway grating.

"I had onions at lunch. I had garlic dressing at dinner. But he'll never know, because I stay kissing sweet, the new Dazzledent way."

A MEGAWATT SMILE SELLS DAZZLEDENT TOOTHPASTE ON TELEVISION EVERY OTHER WEEK.

When the surface is scratched, her words contain sound logic.

"I wouldn't be lying on the floor in the middle of the night in some man's apartment drinking champagne if he wasn't married."

On marriage: *"Getting married?! . . . that'd be worse than living at the club. Then I'd have to start getting in by one o'clock again."*

Richard: *"Very true. You probably would. At least occasionally."*

IN RICHARD'S APARTMENT, THE GIRL GIVES A DEMONSTRATION OF HOW SHE PERFORMS HER COMMERCIAL.

*"A married man.
Air-conditioning.
Champagne and potato chips.
It's just a wonderful party!"*

"WOULD YOU MIND FASTENING MY STRAPS IN THE BACK?
. . . POTATO CHIPS, CHAMPAGNE . . . "

A Chaste Romance

Richard Sherman's summer "affair" begins with a crash. The tomato plant from the apartment above slams down onto his patio, destroying a chair and nearly Richard himself, if he had not moved a few seconds earlier. His understandable annoyance vanishes instantly when he sees who is to blame—the platinum blonde he had let into the building earlier in the evening. Before long, Richard is convinced he is running amok. Only The Girl upstairs can see him through the crisis, and send him racing to join his wife in Maine with newfound confidence in his animal magnetism.

THE GIRL EXPLAINS WHAT MAKES "A REALLY INTERESTING MAN."

"Chopsticks! I can play that too! Shove over."

Musical Interludes

Only in his dreams . . .

*"It shakes me.
It quakes me. It makes me
feel goose-pimply all over."*

Outside of Richard's daydreams, the film's *second* piano concerto, "Chopsticks," rather than Rachmaninoff's composition, is what excites The Girl.

OBLIVIOUS TO ALL AROUND HER, SHE DOESN'T REALIZE RICHARD IS ABOUT TO MAKE HIS MOVE.

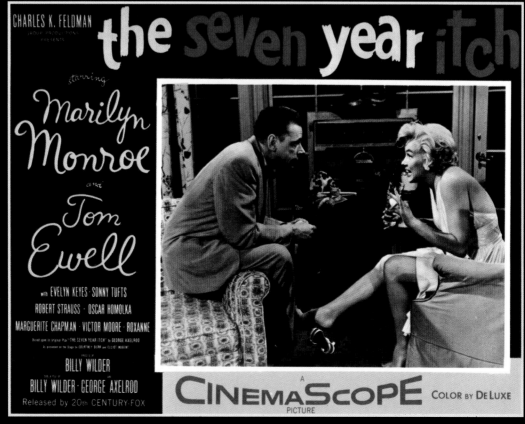

HOW CAN SHE GET OUT OF RICHARD'S APARTMENT IN THE MORNING WITHOUT GIVING PEOPLE THE WRONG IDEA ABOUT THEIR RELATIONSHIP? HER SUGGESTION, "I CAN GET UP AT SIX AND SNEAK UPSTAIRS," IS QUICKLY NIXED BY RICHARD.

Like Potato Chips and Champagne

Marilyn and Tom Ewell had a delicious chemistry that was often missing from the relationships between Marilyn and her leading men. When Fox was casting the male lead of *The Seven Year Itch*, Walter Matthau made a fine test, but the studio decided against taking a chance on a newcomer. Billy Wilder was able to convince them to hire Tom Ewell, however, who had originated the role on Broadway opposite Vanessa Brown. This was unusual in itself, as the common practice was to replace stage actors with well-known movie names. Choosing Ewell over a handsome leading man gave the film the added dimension of placing an average guy opposite an authentic fantasy girl. Together, as The Girl might say, they were like potato chips with champagne.

"I think you're just elegant."

Tips to Beat the Heat . . .

The hot, summertime setting was a central element of the story.

When refrigerating undergarments is not enough, a girl has to devise new strategies.

The Girl discovers a hazard of trying to sleep in a tub of cold water.

To stop an annoying drip, she jams her big toe up the faucet.

Richard: "I guess that's what they call American know-how."

When it gets stuck, a professional is called in:

"There I was with a perfectly strange plumber . . . and no polish on my toenails."

WITH HER FAITHFUL PLUMBER (VICTOR MOORE)

Electric fans can prove tricky as well . . .

"Maybe if I took the little fan, put it in the icebox, and left the icebox door open, then left the bedroom door open, then soak the sheets and pillowcase in ice-water . . . no, that's too icky."

When all else fails, she decides to share an apartment with a close friend who has air-conditioning.

AFTER TAKING UP THE BOARD THAT SEPARATES HER APARTMENT FROM RICHARD'S — "WE CAN DO THIS ALL SUMMER. HMM?"

Marilyn is buzzed in the door and ready to shoot her scenes carrying the much-discussed little fan.

Her refreshing soak in the tub.

Subway gratings also help . . .

The Skirt Scene

The post-midnight hours of September 15, 1954, outside of the Trans-Lux Theater near 52nd Street on Lexington Avenue, a luminous Marilyn wearing a white pleated halter dress, stepped over a subway grating. With a crew member operating a powerful fan positioned below the grille, the stage was set for a legendary scene. Hordes of reporters and spectators (estimates range from several hundred to five thousand) watched the crew film take after take of a history-making moment.

The postscript is that the film of this New York sequence was unusable. Her skirt had flown up to her waist, and the cheers of the crowd were clearly audible. The famous scene's true setting was the controlled atmosphere of a 20th Century-Fox soundstage. Unlike the iconic images that exist, in the finished film Marilyn's skirt billows up only slightly above her knees and a full-body shot is never shown.

Back in New York, a fifty-two foot high picture of The Girl with the upswept skirt was mounted above the marquee of Loew's State Theater at Times Square.

"Oh, do you feel the breeze from the subway?

Isn't it delicious?"

"Ooh! Here comes another one."

A couple of The Girl's lines to Richard that were cut by the censors:

"This one's even cooler—must be an express. Don't you wish you had a skirt? I feel so sorry for you in those hot pants."

"It TICKLES and TANTALIZES!
The funniest comedy since laughter began!"

In addition to the base cost of the film rights to Axelrod's play, the studio paid $175,000 to the playwright and the stage producers to move the opening date of the film up from February 1956. (Its release was supposed to be held until after any New York or touring companies of the play completed their runs.) The premiere was held on June 1, 1955. A radiant birthday girl, just turned twenty-nine and again in white, attended on the arm of Joe DiMaggio, though the couple had separated in October of the previous year.

The price tag on *The Seven Year Itch* was just under two million dollars. It earned back several times that amount for Fox, becoming the studio's most successful film of the year. Marilyn was the biggest star in the world, and she was about to walk away from it all.

910-X-119

Final retakes for *The Seven Year Itch* were shot on January 9, 1955. Two days earlier Marilyn had been in New York. There at a press conference held at the East 64th Street home of her lawyer, Frank Delaney, the announcement of the formation of Marilyn Monroe Productions was made, and a drawn-out dispute between Marilyn and her home studio ensued.

After *The Seven Year Itch*, Fox offered Marilyn *How to Be Very, Very Popular* and *The Revolt of Mamie Stover*, both of which she declined. In the former, Betty Grable and Sheree North starred as empty-headed strippers, and in the latter, Jane Russell played the Honolulu prostitute of the title. Behind the scenes Marilyn and her business partner, photographer Milton Greene, worked to establish their own production company in the hope of obtaining for Marilyn the creative control over her projects that would lead her career in the direction she wanted it to take; not necessarily away from comedies or musicals, but toward roles of greater substance to be developed with the finest talents in the business.

Though she was away from the cameras, 1955 was a momentous, life and career altering year for Marilyn. While her future with Fox was being negotiated by her representatives, she relocated to New York. In preparation for the parts she

"The thing I'd like most is to become a real actress."

—MARILYN, 1955

planned to play in the future, Marilyn dedicated herself to studying her art, first with the celebrated British actress Constance Collier, and then in February she began her association with Lee Strasberg. The head of the acclaimed Actors Studio saw great talent in Marilyn. For months, he and his wife, Paula Strasberg, gave Marilyn private lessons at the family home. Later she sat in on classes at the Actors Studio, where Method acting was practiced, and commenced psychoanalysis as part of her training.

Retaining all the charisma that made her a star and adding an even more touching dimension that was distinctly suited to the cinema, Marilyn's acting was changed forever. As was her life. Lee Strasberg became Marilyn's mentor; Paula Strasberg became her devoted personal acting coach. Meanwhile, in New York Marilyn also became reacquainted and fell in love with the man she would soon marry, Pulitzer Prize-winning playwright Arthur Miller.

The end of Marilyn's yearlong stay in New York was marked by a new contract with Fox, dated December 31, 1955. Taking a year to negotiate, the agreement marked a serious break in the studio system, granting her a combination of independence and control that was almost unheard of for a performer before that time. Among the terms stipulated in her non-exclusive agreement were that she was to make four films for Fox over the course of seven years, for which she was to be paid $100,000 each, plus $500 per week, and an annual retainer. Of greater importance to Marilyn, she also had director, cinematographer, and script approval. She was now ready to return to Hollywood.

THE VIEW FROM EAST 61ST STREET, THE MELANCHOLY MOOD BELYING THE CONFIDENCE WITH WHICH SHE WOULD
EMBARK UPON HER JOURNEY TOWARD INDEPENDENCE.

Marilyn arrived back in Los Angeles from New York in late February 1956 to begin work on *Bus Stop*, a film version of the play by William Inge that opened on Broadway in 1955 starring Kim Stanley as Cherie—the role Marilyn would inherit. Her approved director was Joshua Logan and the screenplay was by George Axelrod. *The Seven Year Itch* writer had gotten to know Marilyn and injected a bit of her own story into his adaptation of the Inge play.

The "new" Marilyn had authority like never before on her films, and she used it to ensure realism in the look of the production. Shown some of the studio's ideas for Cherie's wardrobe, she immediately vetoed the entire lot as unsuited to the character. Going through the wardrobe department, Marilyn pulled a number of shabby items, including a worn black skirt, a tarnished gold lamé jacket with tattered fur trim, a black skirt that had seen better days, and fishnet stockings with runs in them. Further demonstrating commitment to the character, she appeared in unglamorous makeup and lighting designed by Milton Greene to give her the pallid look of a barroom singer who kept late hours and saw sunlight only when dragged out of doors during the day by a forceful cowboy.

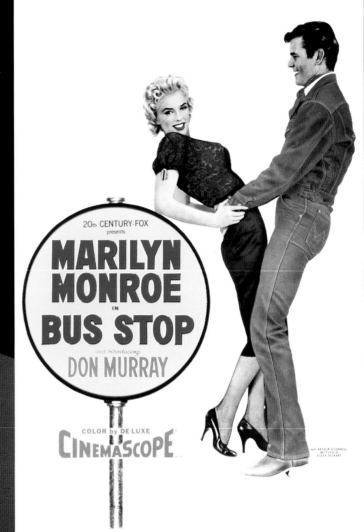

WITH DON MURRAY

CHERIE SHOOS A PRECOCIOUS BOY (TERRY KELMAN) OUT OF THE LADIES ROOM.

Searching for an Angel

Bo Decker (Don Murray) and his best friend and father figure, Virge (Arthur O'Connell), are off to Phoenix by bus for the rodeo. It is only twenty-one-year-old Bo's second time off their Montana ranch, so in addition to competing in every event, Virge decides it is about time Bo found himself a girl. The idea appeals to Bo, but with characteristic over-enthusiasm, no ordinary gal will do; he intends to rope himself "a real hootenanny of an angel."

The night they arrive in Phoenix, Bo finds Cherie, the singer at a local bar. One look is all it takes. Bo aims to marry Cherie and take her back to his ranch by any means necessary. Cherie is attracted to the handsome Bo, but is appalled by his manners. The fragile woman is no match for this force of nature. After walking away with first honors at the rodeo, it is time for Bo and Virge to head home—with Cherie, naturally. Virge helps her attempt to flee by bus to Los Angeles but at the station, Bo lassoes Cherie, ropes her in, and sets her beside him on the bus headed to Montana instead.

There is no chance for Cherie to escape as they drive along the deserted highway. A snowstorm forces them to spend a night at the first bus stop, Grace's Diner. To put an end to Bo's boorish treatment of Cherie, Virge has brawny bus driver Carl (Robert Bray) beat some sense into the cowboy. After losing a fight in front of Cherie, Bo figuratively turns the corner. In the morning he is mellowed, ready to make apologies and express his emotions to Cherie. Feeling the true love and respect from Bo that she has longed for, Cherie can dream of nothing better than to marry and live on a ranch in the arms of her beau.

"For a weddin' present I'm gonna get you a deep freeze, or an electric washer, or any other major appliance ya want!"

BO PAINTS A PICTURE OF LIFE ON THE RANCH FOR CHERIE.

VIRGE, CHERIE, AND BO AT THE BLUE DRAGON.

CHERIE TRIES TO TELL BO "GOODBYE FOREVER."

CARL, THE BUS DRIVER, STEPS IN TO HELP A LADY IN DISTRESS.

"You might say that this line here is the history of my life up 'til now."

The Chantooze

The girl from River Gulch, Arkansas is headed straight as an arrow for Los Angeles to "be somebody." From a talent contest she came away with second prize and an aim in life—to become a great chanteuse. Like her idol, Hildegarde, she needs only one name, Cherie. The Blue Dragon Café is not her idea of a showcase for her singing but it will do until she earns enough money to continue westward to California. In addition to performing the floorshow at the Blue Dragon, she is forced to sweet talk the customers into buying drinks and must tolerate their pinches and grabs. Regrettably, Cherie doesn't have the gift to fascinate an audience from the stage. She is fond of Bo in their first encounter as he makes the crowd pay attention, but to Cherie the dreamer, winding up at his ranch in East No Place, Montana is her worst nightmare.

Perhaps what Cherie desires above all else is respect. Straightforward, she can't lie or keep anything from Bo about the number of boyfriends she has had in the face of his total lack of experience. When Bo ultimately proves he respects Cherie in spite of her past, everything falls into place so that she can drop her unfulfilled dreams of fame without an ounce of regret.

CHERIE CLOSES HER EYES AND ESCAPES HER STUFFY DRESSING ROOM MOMENTARILY.

California Dreaming

Cherie: *"And look where I'm goin'."*

Vera: *"Where?"*

Cherie: *"Hollywood and Vine! Look—straight as an arrow. River Gulch. Hollywood and Vine!"*

Vera: *"What happens when ya get there?"*

Cherie: *"What happens, honey? Ya get discovered, ya get tested, with options, and everything! And you get treated with a little respect too!"*

Cherie believes that making it in Hollywood brings instant respect, the lines containing more than a hint of irony coming from an actress who fully understood what a long, hard fight attaining respect in the movie business would be, especially for a woman, especially one established as a sex symbol.

VERA SEES CHERIE OFF AS SHE ESCAPES BO THROUGH HER DRESSING ROOM WINDOW. CHERIE EXPECTS THIS TO BE THE LAST LEG OF HER JOURNEY TO HOLLYWOOD AND VINE.

Casting Calls

Cherie: In the unthinkable event Marilyn became unavailable to play Cherie, Fox had in mind two backup

blondes: Sheree North and Kim Novak.

Bo Decker: Rock Hudson was the first choice. As Fox accurately guessed they would be unable to get him, a list of

alternatives was compiled, among them Jack Lemmon, Robert Wagner, Aldo Ray, Dale Robertson,

Jeffrey Hunter, Anthony Franciosa, Tony Curtis, Paul Newman, Keith Andes (Marilyn's *Clash By Night*

leading man), Anthony Perkins, Robert Stack, Andy Griffith, and John Kerr. Penciled in far down on

the list was the name of Don Murray (just above Clint Eastwood).

Virgil Blessing: Arthur O'Connell was the first choice for the role of Virgil. He had just worked for Logan as Howard

Bevans in *Picnic*.

Grace: Maureen Stapleton, Ann Sheridan, Ann Sothern, Glenda Farrell, Gloria Grahame, Ann Dvorak,

Barbara Stanwyck. Subsequently the choices were narrowed to Stapleton and Betty Field, who was

selected for the part.

WITH ARTHUR O'CONNELL AND DON MURRAY. VIRGE CAN'T REASON WITH BO ONCE HIS MIND IS MADE UP.

Two Locations and a Wedding

Filming took place at Fox, as well as on location in hot Phoenix, Arizona and frigid Sun Valley, Idaho. Marilyn came down with a throat infection after the Sun Valley shoot and was admitted to St. Vincent Hospital in Los Angeles, where she spent four days in mid-April treated for acute bronchitis.

Bus Stop gave a pair of skilled newcomers their start. Don Murray, a stage and television actor with the right looks and build, was chosen by the director to make his film debut in the role of Bo Dekker. Hope Lange, also making her debut, was cast as Elma. During a break in the middle of production, while Marilyn was in the hospital with bronchitis, Murray and Lange used the time to be married on April 14, 1956.

RODEO SCENES WERE SHOT ON LOCATION IN PHOENIX.

MARILYN ATTEMPTS TO KEEP OUT THE SUN VALLEY COLD.

JOSHUA LOGAN GIVES COUNSEL TO HIS STAR PRIOR TO FILMING A PARTICULARLY EMOTIONAL SEQUENCE.

Star and Director

Joshua Logan, acclaimed for his mounting of the stage production of *South Pacific*, had just filmed another William Inge play, *Picnic*. Logan got along well with Marilyn. It helped that he established alternate shooting schedules to accommodate her inevitable late arrivals to the set. As Marilyn was well-known for requiring numerous takes, Logan developed an unusual approach to working with her in one particularly long scene set on the bus. Instead of yelling "Cut" constantly, Logan loaded film in his camera, pointed it at Marilyn, and let her go. If she fumbled a line, he let her find her way back and edited as needed later.

THE MOVING BREAKTHROUGH SCENE BETWEEN MARILYN AND DON MURRAY AT GRACE'S DINER.

A Word from the Censors...

Virgil should tell Bo, "It's time you went down to the city and met up with a gal," rather than "got yourself a gal."

Bo's lines about Cherie being the first girl he ever "had anything to do with" should be handled with delicacy.

The original ending had to be modified as it seemed too overt that Virge and Grace would begin an affair out of wedlock.

The role of the boy on the bus, played by Terry Kelman, was originally much larger. Named Gerald, he was involved in several comedy scenes in a bus station restroom, on the bus, and at Grace's. Something of another Henry Spofford III (of *Gentlemen Prefer Blondes*), only less of a little gentleman, the Hays Office felt the precocious boy showed an appreciation for Cherie too mature for his age. In the end, he interacts with Cherie only briefly.

WITH TERRY KELMAN (RIGHT) IN ONE AMONG MANY SCENES THAT DIDN'T MAKE THE FINAL PRINT OF *BUS STOP*.

From the Cutting Room Floor

Logan was forced to make many cuts to *Bus Stop*. Following are some of the discarded scenes.

After Bo barges into Cherie's room at 9 a.m., waking her up after only four hours sleep with a recitation of the Gettysburg Address, he takes her out to breakfast. This scene in a restaurant near the stockyards had a flabbergasted Cherie learning Bo's breakfast of choice: three raw hamburgers with a thick slice of onion and some piccalilli—and a quart of milk beside.

There was an attempt to stage a wedding at the rodeo after Cherie tries to flee the arena while Bo ropes a steer. In the final cut, she successfully escapes and the scene ends. The initial plan was for her to be stopped by the two *Life* magazine reporters, who have gotten wind of the planned wedding. Hoping for a good angle to their story on the rodeo, they prove Cherie's undoing by asking her to pause to pose for a picture. In the momentary delay, she is besieged by people with flowers and cakes, a preacher, Bo, and a group of spectators. Finally, the crowd becomes so large that Cherie is able to sneak away in their midst.

The "upstairs" room of Grace's above the restaurant that is referred to several times by Carl, the bus driver, was originally the setting of a sequence in which Cherie, looking for a bed for the two children, takes them upstairs, and walks in on a cozy scene between Grace and Carl. They are rattled by the interruption but Cherie pushes forward. In Grace's bedroom, Cherie tucks in the children. As they nod off, Cherie is engrossed in what is an odd choice for the kids' bedtime story—a selection from *Love Confessions*. "His lean, bronzed fingers stroked my cheek. I fought it! Oh! How I fought it . . ."

A reference to the scene remains in the final film. In the morning after the snowstorm at Grace's, Cherie says, "I musta read myself to sleep. Such an interesting story."

WITH TERRY KELMAN AND LINDA BRACE. CHERIE READS THE KIDS A BEDTIME STORY——AND GETS MORE PLEASURE OUT OF IT THAN THEY DO.

A Girl's Best Friend

Vera is Cherie's first real girl friend. She was played by Eileen Heckart, who had just finished playing in Arthur Miller's *A View from the Bridge*. She and Marilyn became friends. In this scene that was cut from the final film, Vera gives Bo the encouragement that leads to Cherie's being "abducted."

Vera: "And what's she gonna do? Wanderin' around on street corners waitin' to be discovered . . . Sing? She can't even hustle drinks! She can't do nothin' good 'cept make some man happy . . . like you! That's what she needs! Somebody to take care of her! Somebody big and strong . . . with a ranch!"

Virge: "Now wait a minute, lady."

Vera: "Can't ya understand? You two was meant for each other! What are ya waitin' fer! Git down to that bus station, drag her off to that bus, pick her up on your horse and ride away with her to East No Place, Montana, where she belongs!"

"I'M SO DRY I'M SPITTIN' COTTON." VERA FEEDS HER FRIEND THE LINE GUARANTEED TO GET ANY PATRON OF THE BLUE DRAGON TO BUY HER A DRINK.

Marilyn's exceptional performance was overlooked by the Academy. The missed nomination may have been, as Marilyn believed, the result of the most significant cut of all, the deletion of an extended version of the scene she played with Hope Lange, in which Cherie opens up about her past and shares her insights on life and love. Sections in blue were cut from the final film:

Cherie: "I don't know why I keep expectin' myself to fall in love, but I do."

Elma: "I know I expect to, some day."

Cherie: "I'm seriously beginnin' to wonder if there's a kind of love I have in mind. . . . naturally, I'd like to get married and have a family and all them things but . . . "

Elma: "But you've never been in love?"

Cherie: "I don't know. Maybe I have and I didn't know it. That's what I mean. Maybe I don't know what love is. Maybe I'm expectin' it to be somethin' it ain't. I just feel that, regardless how crazy ya are 'bout some guy, ya gotta feel . . . and it's hard to put into words, but . . . ya gotta feel he respects ya. Yeah, that's what I mean. . . . I just gotta feel that whoever I marry has some real regard for me aside from all that, lovin' stuff. You know what I mean?"

Elma: "I think so. What will ya do when ya get to Los Angeles?"

Cherie: "I don't know. Maybe if I don't get discovered right away, I could get me a job on one of the radio stations there. Even singin' hillbilly if I have to. Or else, I can always go to work in Liggett's or Walgreen's. Then after a while I'll prob'ly marry some guy, whether I think I love him or not. Who am I to keep insistin' I should fall in love? You hear all about love when you're a kid and just take it for granted that such a thing really exists. Maybe ya have to find out for yourself it don't. Maybe everyone's afraid to tell ya."

CHERIE FINDS IT IMPOSSIBLE TO SLEEP THROUGH THE GETTYSBURG ADDRESS.

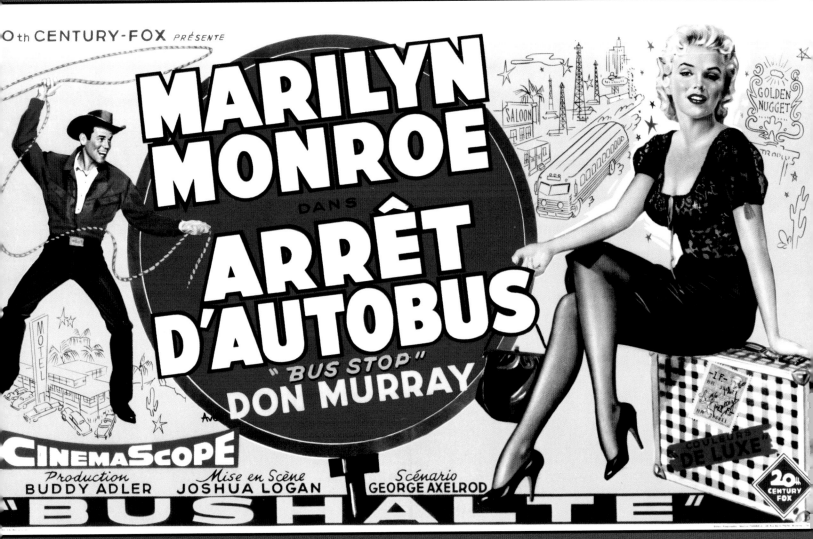

FRENCH POSTER FOR *BUS STOP*

Praise for the Actress

Marilyn's work in *Bus Stop* earned her some of the best reviews of her career. In her sustained performance, every move she made was in character, and the Southern accent maintained consistency. Marilyn's subtle, luminous method captured on film in close-ups was moving from the humorous beginnings to the last few moments with Bo after Cherie has fallen in love and is happy to go with him to Montana; she purrs in his arms as she feels the warmth of his love in his wool-lined coat.

"Well, CHERRY, you're liable to freeze to death in that skimpy little thing."

A COWBOY AND A GENTLEMAN TAKES HIS HAT OFF TO THE WOMAN HE LOVES.

The Rocky Road to Love

BOY MEETS GIRL.

BOY LOSES GIRL.

BOY TRIES TO WIN GIRL BACK.

"I'D GO ANYWHERE IN THE WORLD WITH YOU NOW."

Bo: *"I like ya the way ya are, so what do I care how ya got that way?"*

Cherie: *"That's the sweetest, tenderest thing anyone ever said to me."*

"I'd like for you to kiss me Beau."

TENDERNESS WINS CHERIE'S HEART.

Time Away

Marilyn's contract with Fox was non-exclusive, and prior to *Bus Stop*, her next project had already been scheduled. It would be a Marilyn Monroe Production released by Warner Bros. In July 1956, Marilyn and her new husband, Arthur Miller, arrived in England, where she made *The Prince and the Showgirl* with Laurence Olivier. For her performance Marilyn won Italy's David di Donatello Award and she was nominated for a British Academy Award.

Fox subsequently anticipated her return in a remake of *The Blue Angel* co-starring Spencer Tracy, but the project fell through. In 1958, both *The Sound and the Fury* and *Can-Can* failed to interest Mrs. Marilyn Miller, who was based on the east coast with her husband at their homes in New York and Connecticut. In the fall of that year she made a brilliant film by Billy Wilder that she could not pass up, *Some Like it Hot*.

In the intervening years, Fox attempted to fill the void left by Marilyn's absence by starring Sheree North and Jayne Mansfield in comedies like *The Lieutenant Wore Skirts*, *The Girl Can't Help It*, and *Will Success Spoil Rock Hunter?*. In late 1959, Marilyn was finally set to return to the Fox lot, where she hoped to make a worthy follow-up to the hugely successful *Some Like it Hot*.

DURING THE MAKING OF *LET'S MAKE LOVE*.

··· Looking for a Billionaire

Let's Make Love came to Marilyn via producer Jerry Wald as *The Billionaire*, a comedy script written by Norman Krasna (reportedly with Yul Brynner in mind as the title character). There were delays getting the film into production and preparing a satisfactory screenplay so that by November 1959, when Marilyn began preliminary work on the film, she had no

leading man. Wald's search for her co-star was exhaustive. Brynner himself, Gregory Peck, Cary Grant, Charlton Heston, Rock Hudson, and James Stewart all declined for various reasons. When Arthur Miller suggested Yves Montand with Marilyn's backing, and the actor accepted the part, Fox executives could breathe again for the time being. Montand was a French star just making his mark stateside with his successful one-man show, *An Evening with Yves Montand.* The co-stars would be acting under George Cukor. Marilyn had never worked with the acclaimed director but his participation was a promising sign for the film, and they began shooting on January 18, 1960.

Millers and Montands

Fox Publicity threw a cocktail party for Yves Montand on January 15, 1960, in honor of his arrival in Hollywood. Montand and his wife, actress Simone Signoret, had played John and Elizabeth Proctor in French stage and screen productions of Miller's *The Crucible*. The two couples rented adjacent bungalows at the Beverly Hills Hotel and became firm friends until both Miller and Signoret were called out of town. Left alone without their spouses, Marilyn and Montand had a dalliance that was well-known within the industry during the short time it lasted.

WORD QUICKLY SPREAD THAT THE STARS' ROMANCE CARRIED ON OFF THE SCREEN.

MARILYN FILMS A ROMANTIC SCENE WITH YVES MONTAND, OBSERVED INTENTLY BY A CREWMEMBER AND CHOREOGRAPHER JACK COLE (RIGHT).

· On the Set Celebrations ·

EASTER BUNNY CAKE FOR THE COMPANY—MARILYN WITH DIRECTOR GEORGE CUKOR.

YVES MONTAND HELPS MARILYN CELEBRATE HER BIRTHDAY ON JUNE 1, 1960.

A Husband's Help

The filming of *Let's Make Love* was prolonged and Miller left his wife to her co-star during production because he had plans to meet with director John Huston in Ireland to work on the script of *The Misfits*, the film Marilyn was scheduled to make whenever the seemingly interminable *Let's Make Love* was completed. The most significant of the delays was caused by an actors' and writers' strike occurring at a time when the troubled production was in desperate need of rewrites. Miller came back to Hollywood to act as script doctor on his wife's film.

ARTHUR MILLER WAS ON HAND IN THE EARLY DAYS OF PRODUCTION. HERE HE WATCHES MARILYN ABSORB INSTRUCTION FROM GEORGE CUKOR.

"You can always tell an outsider"

Jean-Marc: *"How?"*

Amanda: *"Mostly the way they look at girls in rehearsal clothes."*

Jean-Marc: *"How do people in show business look?"*

Amanda: *"They don't. I mean, a girl can walk around backstage with nothing on except her good will—and nobody will even turn his head. The same girl, fully dressed walks down an aisle of clerks in an office— pinched black and blue. What's the matter with you people anyway?"*

MARILYN AS AMANDA DELL ENTICES "OUTSIDER" JEAN-MARC IN HER REHEARSAL CLOTHES.

The Billionaire

Jean-Marc Clement (Yves Montand), a billionaire descended from six generations of moneyed rogues, learns from his public relations council (Tony Randall) that a Greenwich Village theatrical troupe is planning to satirize him in an upcoming revue. Hoping to remove the sting of being ridiculed by laughing along with them, Jean-Marc attends a rehearsal where he is captivated by the star of the show, Amanda Dell (Marilyn). Unlike most women Jean-Marc encounters, she does not fall at his feet, leading him to wonder if he can earn her love without the aid of his money and name. Posing as "Alexander Dumas," a costume jewelry salesman and struggling actor, he takes the part of the phony Jean-Marc Clement in the show.

Amanda is friendly to Jean-Marc, but not any more than she is with her co-star, Tony Danton (Frankie Vaughan). If he must be a star to gain her attention, Jean-Marc will hire the best teachers imaginable. With comic routines from Milton Berle, singing lessons by Bing Crosby, and dance instruction from Gene Kelly—not to mention having one of his own men buy controlling interest in the show—Jean-Marc is handed all of Tony's big routines. Knowing the show means everything to Tony, Amanda conspires to have him reinstated, whereupon Jean-Marc uses his power to close down the production.

"Alexander" convinces Amanda that her personal plea to Clement is their only hope of reopening the show. By now Jean-Marc has asked Amanda to marry him and told her who he is. She loves him but thinks he is insane. At Clement's office, she learns the truth for herself. When Amanda recovers from the shock, Jean-Marc has the girl of his dreams—the one who fell in love with him when he was "poor."

AMANDA, ACCOMPANIED BY JEAN-MARC, PUBLICITY MAN ALEXANDER COFFMAN (TONY RANDALL),
LAWYER JOHN WALES (WILFRID HYDE-WHITE), AND PRODUCER OLIVER BURTON (DAVID BURNS),
PREPARES TO GO INTO ACTION TO SAVE HER SHOW.

AMANDA PERFORMS WITH TONY, PLAYED BY FRANKIE VAUGHAN.

"Hey You with the Crazy Eyes"

*"There used to be an actor. He played Abraham Lincoln for so many years—
this is true—he grew his own beard. He went around in a shawl.
And you know what they used to say? He looks like Lincoln.
He talks like Lincoln. But he would not be satisfied 'til he gets shot!"*

FROM HIS ACTING, TO HIS SINGING, TO HIS MENTAL STATE,
AMANDA IS GREATLY CONCERNED ABOUT HER NEW FRIEND.

Amanda Dell

Sweet as candy and twice as appealing, Amanda the performer is a preacher's daughter, deeply sympathetic to her friends as well as to four million strangers in Haiti who live on twenty-five dollars a week. She is also sensitive about her own inadequacies and wants to be respected. ("I can't stand anyone who makes fun of me.") Accordingly, she takes her work seriously and is enrolled in classes to improve her mind, even passing on dates to get in extra rehearsals and study time, leaving suitors like Jean-Marc and Tony unsure of where they stand. Amanda detests being lied to, so when she finds out the true identity of "Alexander" she is quick to anger but her love is sufficient to extinguish these hurt feelings. In spite of herself, Amanda's heart belongs to a billionaire.

WATCHING JEAN-MARC PERFORM

THE TRUTH ABOUT ALEXANDER DAWNS ON AMANDA.

"The least you could've done is tell me who you are!"

Jean-Marc: *"I did tell you."*

Amanda: *"How did you expect me to believe it?"*

Jean-Marc: *"Because it's true."*

Amanda: *"That's no excuse."*

WHEN THEY FIRST MEET, AMANDA, LIKE EVERYONE ELSE AT THE THEATER, MISTAKES JEAN-MARC FOR A DOWN-AND-OUT ACTOR LOOKING FOR A JOB.

Twenty-three Years Earlier

Let's Make Love was a substantially reworked version of the 1937 picture *On the Avenue*, which starred Dick Powell, Madeleine Carroll, and Alice Faye. In the earlier film it was the girl who had all the money in the world and the man was the performer having fun at her expense in a musical comedy production.

AMANDA TRIES TO HELP JEAN-MARC ALONG AS HE STRUGGLES THROUGH REHEARSALS.

(LEFT) CONTACT SHEET OF MARILYN REHEARSING WITH JACK COLE. DIRECTOR GEORGE CUKOR IS ALSO PICTURED IN A FEW OF THE SHOTS.

Marilyn and Jack Cole

Marilyn worked with her favorite choreographer, Jack Cole, for the final time on *Let's Make Love*. Cole had done well

by a number of the leading screen goddesses of the day, including Rita Hayworth, Marlene Dietrich, Betty Grable,

and Lana Turner. During filming he would guide performers with his off-camera movements which they mimicked

before the camera. Marilyn trusted him since *Gentlemen Prefer Blondes* and subsequently worked with him on *River*

of No Return, *There's No Business Like Show Business*, and *Some Like it Hot*. They worked tirelessly on her numbers for

Let's Make Love, highlighted by his staging of "My Heart Belongs to Daddy." Marilyn knew it had been a trying expe-

rience. She apologized to Cole with a gift of $2,000, which she asked that he spend on a well-deserved vacation.

"My Heart Belongs to Daddy" in Rehearsals

MARILYN AND THE CHORUS BOYS FOLLOW JACK COLE'S CHOREOGRAPHY.

"My Heart Belongs to Daddy" in Performance

MARILYN'S FIRST MOMENTS IN *LET'S MAKE LOVE* WERE ALSO HER BEST IN THE FILM. SHE SLIDES INTO VIEW FROM POLES ABOVE THE SET, DIRECTLY INTO HER NUMBER.

"Let's Make Love"

MARILYN AND YVES MONTAND PERFORM THE "LET'S MAKE LOVE" NUMBER.

"Specialization"

MARILYN'S AMANDA EXPLAINS THE IMPORTANCE OF "SPECIALIZATION."

To Be Wonderful

Set inside a cab before Jean-Marc drops Amanda off at her father's church, the scene in which Marilyn's character gets to open up and talk about her dreams was cut from the film. The exchange was also intended to be the point at which Amanda and Jean-Marc first connect on a personal level. Its omission left no other scene that effectively served this purpose. A portion of the sequence is reproduced here.

STARRY-EYED AMANDA

Asked by Jean-Marc what she wants in life, Amanda answers:

> *Amanda:*   *"Well, I'd like to be wonderful. . . . I guess to entertain people. . . . "*
> *Jean-Marc:* *"People. Why are they so important?"*

> (He calls them "foolish, perspiring strangers for whom she must work like a slave.)

> *Amanda:*   *"Oh, I don't know, but when those foolish, perspiring strangers sit down together in a theater, and you're good that night, and everything starts coming out the way it should—something comes back from them that, kind of lifts you a little off the ground. It's like you're not just you any more, not a stranger; like—they all melt together and you're—at home. Like in a family. I can't explain it, but once you've felt it happen, there's nothing like it in the world."*

JEAN-MARC DOESN'T UNDERSTAND AMANDA, BUT HE LOVES TO BE WITH HER.

Mugging for the Camera

Postscript

Marilyn celebrated her thirty-fourth birthday on the set as principal photography neared its finish. The production went well over budget, increasing the difficulty of its turning a profit. Released on September 8, 1960, expectations ran high for the CinemaScope musical comedy, but it would become one of Marilyn's least successful pictures.

MARILYN'S ENTRANCE AS ELLEN ARDEN.

···That Certain Something

It was the early months of 1962. Marilyn was still the World's Film Favorite and in March she collected the Golden Globe award that said as much. Marilyn was now set to begin what would have been her thirtieth film, and her twentieth Fox Picture. Since *Let's Make Love*, she had made one film away from her home studio, *The Misfits*. Following completion of the black-and-white film, Marilyn was away from the screen for a year. *Something's Got to Give* would return her to the screen in Fox's full color, CinemaScope glory at a time when the studio sorely needed a box office sensation.

George Cukor, Marilyn's *Let's Make Love* director, had been signed for the production, and she was eager to work with her friend Dean Martin, along with a supporting cast that included Cyd Charisse, Steve Allen, Phil Silvers, two children, and a cocker spaniel.

The Inspiration

Something's Got to Give was to have been a remake of a 1940 RKO comedy that starred Cary Grant and Irene Dunne, *My Favorite Wife*, which itself took inspiration from Alfred Lord Tennyson's poem "Enoch Arden." The attempts of several writers to rework the original Academy Award-nominated story proved problematic. Among the writers brought in was Nunnally Johnson, who had written the screenplay of *How to Marry a Millionaire*. Between the efforts of Johnson, Cukor, and Walter Bernstein, a shooting script for *Something's Got to Give* crystallized.

One More Time

My Favorite Wife—and *Something's Got to Give*—reemerged in 1963 as *Move Over Darling*. The original script was again reworked, by Hal Kanter and Jack Sher, and Doris Day was cast opposite James Garner.

In Production

Marilyn reported for filming for the first time on April 30, 1962, though shooting had begun a week earlier. But she was diagnosed with acute sinusitis and suffered from fevers and infection throughout the production schedule. This, coupled with her fear that the effects of illness would detract from her performance, caused many absences and expensive production delays. Meanwhile, Fox's financial situation was desperate. In addition to massive cost overruns on their epic production of *Cleopatra*, they, like all of the film studios, were trying to cope with general upheavals taking place in the industry caused by television and the end of the star system. In light of these circumstances, Marilyn was dismissed, and on June 8, *Something's Got to Give* was shut down.

The initial plan was to recast the film—until Dean Martin was informed. With due respect to the actresses to whom Fox offered the part—Kim Novak, Shirley MacLaine, and Lee Remick—as far as Martin was concerned, there was no substitute for Marilyn. By late July there was a complete reversal in Fox's position. Peter Levathes, then head of the studio, personally asked Marilyn to resume production on *Something's Got to Give*. She too was anxious to see the work completed, and on August 1, 1962, Marilyn signed a lucrative new contract with Fox.

Four days later, the world was shocked to learn of Marilyn Monroe's untimely death, caused by an overdose of sleeping pills. The scenes she had shot for *Something's Got to Give* became her last moments on film; with hair more white-blonde than ever and blue eyes sparkling, the thirty-six-year-old superstar's beauty and talent shone bright.

(RIGHT) RADIANT ON ONE OF HER FIRST DAYS ON THE SET

Playing Dress-Up

Marilyn's work on *Something's Got to Give* had a positive beginning when she reported to the studio on April 10 for costume, hair, and makeup tests. Radiant, upbeat, and in command of the camera, the entire company was thrilled.

MARILYN SHOT THIS TEST WEARING A COSTUME PREVIOUSLY SEEN IN *LET'S MAKE LOVE*.

MORE TRIM AND FIT THAN SHE HAD BEEN IN RECENT YEARS, MARILYN'S FIGURE WAS ON DISPLAY AGAIN IN THESE TESTS.

"How long does it take a man to tell a woman that his wife's back?"

The Two Mrs. Ardens

Ellen Wagstaff Arden was serving as the official photographer for a trans-Pacific yacht race when, in a tragic turn of events, she was swept overboard by a twenty-five-foot wave. After an exhaustive search and the passage of five years, Ellen's husband, Nick (Dean Martin), has her declared legally dead. Unbeknownst to her family, Ellen has just been rescued from the island where she was stranded. She returns home to reclaim her position as Nick's wife and mother of their two children—the very day her shocked husband has remarried. The mystified *second* Mrs. Arden, Bianca (Cyd Charisse), vents her frustration about Nick's inexplicable reserve in the bedroom to her badgered psychiatrist, Dr. Schlick (Steve Allen). Though he loves Ellen, Nick can't bring himself to tell Bianca of his wife's return. Their situation is further complicated when Nick learns that Ellen's five years on that South Sea island were spent in the company of Stephen Burkett (Tom Tryon), known to Ellen as "Adam," to her "Eve." To soothe an irate Nick, Ellen enlists a meek shoe salesman to pretend to be Stephen Burkett. With convincing restraint, Nick conceals the fact that he has already seen the handsome, athletic, real Mr. Burkett. He is now more suspicious than ever, but two people as in love as Ellen and Nick have no intention of losing each other again.

"MISS TIC" HELPS THE NEW MR. AND MRS. ARDEN WITH THEIR LUGGAGE.

Ellen Wagstaff Arden

Little did new mother Ellen know that her brief vacation from teething children would turn into five years. Persuasive, provocative, and playful, the lady of the house is back—and not about to let even a strong personality like Bianca Arden take her place.

"Miss Ingrid Tic . . . T-I-C Tic"

NEWLYWEDS NICK AND BIANCA MEET THE KIDS' GORGEOUS NEW NURSE.

The *Something's Got to Give* footage shows that Marilyn chose not to heighten the breathless quality of her voice in this picture, but she did adopt a foreign accent for the only time in her film career—when Ellen poses as a Swedish nurse to the children to explain her presence until Nick can find the right moment to tell his bride about his wife. In *My Favorite Wife*, Irene Dunne's Ellen becomes an animated old friend of Nick's from the South. That too would have made an interesting and funny situation for Marilyn's film. Her Ellen might suddenly have morphed into *Bus Stop*'s Cherie.

"Honeymoon is over? Jah?"

Uncooperative Co-star

A devoted dog remembers its mistress. On May 14, Marilyn shot scenes with a cocker spaniel that in the film was named "Tippy," after the beloved dog she owned as a child. Dog lover that she was, Marilyn remained in high spirits, amused by her canine co-star, as its trainer labored in vain to make the dog take direction.

Playtime

Clearly not a believer in the show business adage that an actor should never work with natural scene-stealers like animals or children, Marilyn was even more jubilant with the children than she had been working with Tippy. She was playing a starring role as a mother for the only time in her career. A woman who for years dreamed of becoming a mother in real life, Marilyn made a particular effort to develop a rapport with the child actors by playing with them prior to their scenes together.

IN SPITE OF THE EFFORTS OF A FRUSTRATED TRAINER AND A CHEERFUL CO-STAR, TIPPY REMAINED UNPREDICTABLE.

"You know what you two kids are? You're my two sweethearts. My two best sweethearts in the whole world!"

ACTING A SCENE WITH ROBERT CHRISTOPHER MORLEY.

A Moonlight Swim

Ellen Arden tries to entice her husband to join her for a dip in the pool.

"Come on. The water's so refreshing"

After returning from her trip to New York, Marilyn slipped into (and later, out of) a flesh-colored bathing suit for her nude swimming sequence. On a closed set, Marilyn splashed, giggled, posed seductively in and around the pool, and made history as the first star to film a nude scene for a major American movie. Photos from the set became magazine features worldwide, including Marilyn's sixth *Life* cover story.

"Happy Birthday, Mr. President"

In the middle of production, Marilyn traveled to New York to attend the birthday gala for President John F. Kennedy held at Madison Square Garden on May 19. It was very important to Marilyn to appear. She had been the guest performer designated to sing "Happy Birthday"—and she did so in the most memorable way conceivable.

ALTHOUGH IT TOOK MANY TAKES TO FILM THESE FEW MOMENTS WITH DEAN MARTIN, IN WHICH ELLEN TRIES TO EXPLAIN WHY A ROMANCE BETWEEN HER AND STEPHEN BIRKETT WAS IMPOSSIBLE, MARTIN REMAINED A GREAT SYMPATHETIC FRIEND TO MARILYN THROUGHOUT.

"Happy Birthday (Suit)"

A considerably more modest birthday celebration was given for Marilyn's thirty-sixth. Featuring a cake that said "Happy Birthday (Suit)," the small party was held on the set at the end of what would be her final day of filming, June 1.

"Will you have lunch with me?"

"I bring my lunch to the store."

"I'd be so grateful if you'd— take it out."

DEAN MARTIN (RIGHT) ALREADY KNOWS WALLY COX IS NOT THE VIRILE STEPHEN BURKETT.

Is He or Isn't He?

A compliant shoe salesman who helps reacquaint Ellen with high heels after five years of bare feet, also attempts

to help her out of trouble with a jealous Nick. She introduces him as Stephen Burkett, the man with whom she

was stranded on the island. On her final day of shooting, Marilyn shot this scene with Dean Martin and Wally Cox

The Reconstruction

In 1999, thirty-seven years after *Something's Got to Give* was shelved, the restoration of perhaps the most famous film that never was began. Nearly nine hours of unedited footage was surfaced from the vaults of 20th Century-Fox and painstakingly restored to its original brilliance. The scenes that could be arranged into a cohesive form resulted in a thirty-seven-minute reconstruction of *Something's Got to Give*. This work was unveiled on June 1, 2001, what would have been Marilyn's seventy-fifth birthday. Through this effort, Marilyn's vast public has the haunting final footage of the ultimate screen goddess to add to the treasury of unforgettable images on film she left behind.

MARILYN'S LAST HURRAH FOR THE MOVIE CAMERA IS CAPTURED ON HER FINAL DAY ON THE SET.

Appendix

Scudda Hoo! Scudda Hay! •———————————————

A 20th Century-Fox Picture (1948)

Walter Morosco (Producer); F. Hugh Herbert (Director and Screenplay) from novel by George Agnew Chamberlain; Ernest Palmer (Photography); Natalie Kalmus (Technicolor Color Consultant), Leonard Doss (Associate); Fred Sersen (Photographic Effects); Cyril Mockridge (Music); Lionel Newman (Musical Director); Herbert Spencer and Earle Hagen (Orchestration); Lyle Wheeler and Albert Hogsett (Art Directors); Thomas Little and Stanley Detlie (Set Decoration); Charles Le Maire (Wardrobe Director); Bonnie Cashin (Costumes); Ben Nye (Makeup); Eugene Grossman and Roger Heman (Sound); Eli Dun and Bert Briskin (Assistant Directors); Harmon Jones (Editor).

Release date: April 14, 1948, Run time: 95 minutes.

Cast: June Haver (Rad McGill); Lon McCallister (Daniel "Snug" Dominy); Walter Brennan (Tony Maule); Anne Revere (Judith Dominy); Natalie Wood (Bean McGill); Robert Karnes (Stretch); Henry Hull (Milt Dominy); Tom Tully (Robert "Roarer" McGill); Geraldine Wall (Mrs. McGill); Ken Christy (Sheriff Bursom); Edward Gargan (Ted); Charles Wagenheim (Barber); Marilyn Monroe (Betty).

Dangerous Years •———————————————

A 20th Century-Fox Picture (1947)

Sol M. Wurtzel (Producer), Howard Sheehan (Associate); Arthur Pierson (Director); Arnold Belgard (Story and Screenplay); Benjamin Kline (Photography); Rudy Schrager (Music); David Chudnow (Musical Director); Walter Koessler (Art Director); Al Greenwood (Set Decoration); Jack Casey (Makeup); Irene Beshon (Hairstylist); Max M. Hutchinson (Sound); Paul Wurtzel (Assistant Director); William Claxton and Frank Baldridge (Editors).

Release date: December 7, 1947, Run time: 62 minutes.

Cast: William Halop (Danny Jones); Scotty Beckett (Willy Miller); Richard Gaines (Edgar Burns); Ann E. Todd (Doris Martin); Jerome Cowan (Weston); Anabel Shaw (Connie Burns); Darryl Hickman (Leo Emerson); Dickie Moore (Gene Spooner); Harry Harvey, Jr. (Phil Kenny); Gil Stratton, Jr. (Tammy McDonald); Harry Shannon (Judge Raymond); Donald Curtis (Jeff Carter); Joseph Vitale (August Miller); Marilyn Monroe (Evie); Nana Bryant (Miss Templeton); Tom Kennedy (Adamson).

Ladies of the Chorus •———————————————

A Columbia Picture (1948)

Harry A. Romm (Producer); Phil Karlson (Director); Joseph Carole and Harry Sauber (Screenplay) from story by Harry Sauber; Frank Redman (Photography); Mischa Bakaleinikoff (Music); Jack Boyle (Dance Director); Robert Peterson (Art Director); James Crowe (Set Decoration); Helen Hunt (Hairstylist); Frank Goodwin (Sound); Carter DeHaven (Assistant Director); Richard Fantl (Editor).

Release date: October 22, 1948, Run time: 61 minutes.

Cast: Adele Jergens (Mae Martin); Marilyn Monroe (Peggy Martin); Rand Brooks (Randy Carroll); Nana Bryant (Mrs. Adele Carroll); Eddie Garr (Billy Mackay); Steven Geray (Salisbury); Bill Edwards (Alan Wakely).

Songs: "The Ladies of the Chorus," "Every Baby Needs a Da Da Daddy," "Anyone Can Tell I Love You," "I'm So Crazy for You," "You're Never Too Old" (Lester Lee and Allan Roberts).

Love Happy

A Mary Pickford Presentation, released by United Artists (1950)

Lester Cowan and Mary Pickford (Producers); David Miller (Director); Frank Tashlin, Mac Benoff, and Ben Hecht (Screenplay) from story by Harpo Marx; William C. Mellor (Photography); Howard A. Anderson (Photographic Effects); Ann Ronnell (Music); Paul J. Smith (Musical Director, Orchestra Conductor); Harry Geller (Orchestration); Billy Daniel (Dance Director); Gabriel Scognamillo (Production Designer); Casey Roberts (Set Decoration); Grace Houston and Norma (Costumes); Richard Bachler (Men's Wardrobe); Scotty Rackin (Hairstylist); Fred Phillips (Makeup); Basil Wrangell and Albrecht Joseph (Editors).

Cast: Groucho Marx (Detective Sam Grunion); Harpo Marx (Harpo); Chico Marx (Faustino); Ilona Massey (Madame Egelichi); Vera-Ellen (Maggie Phillips); Marion Hutton (Bunny Dolan); Raymond Burr (Alphonse Zoto); Melville Cooper (Throckmorton); Paul Valentine (Mike Johnson); Leon Belasco (Mr. Lyons); Eric Blore (Mackinaw); Bruce Gordon (Hannibal Zoto); Marilyn Monroe (Grunion's Client).

Songs: "Love Happy," "Willow Weep for Me" (Ann Ronell); "Who Stole the Jam?" (Ann Ronell, Harold Spina, and Walter Bullock); "Gypsy Love Song" (Victor Herbert); "Swanee River" (Stephen Foster); "Polonaise in A Flat" (Frédéric Chopin).

Release Date: March 3, 1950, Run time: 85 minutes.

A Ticket to Tomahawk

A 20th Century-Fox Picture (1950)

Robert Bassler (Producer); Richard Sale (Director); Mary Loos and Richard Sale (Screenplay); Harry Jackson (Photography); Richard Mueller (Technicolor Color Consultant); Fred Sersen (Photographic Effects); Cyril Mockridge (Music); Lionel Newman (Musical Director); Herbert Spencer and Earle Hagen (Orchestration); Kenny Williams (Dance Director); Lyle Wheeler and George W. Davis (Art Directors); Thomas Little and Fred J. Rode (Set Decoration); Charles Le Maire (Wardrobe Director); Rene Hubert (Costumes); Ben Nye (Makeup); W. D. Flick and Harry M. Leonard (Sound); Henry Weinberger and Joe Richards (Assistant Directors); Harmon Jones (Editor).

Cast: Dan Dailey (Johnny Jameson); Anne Baxter (Kit Dodge); Rory Calhoun (Dakota); Walter Brennan (Terence Sweeny); Charles Kemper (Chuckity Jones); Connie Gilchrist (Madame Adelaide); Arthur Hunnicutt (Sad Eyes Tatum); Will Wright (Marshal Kit Dodge); Chief Yowlachie (Pawnee); Victor Sen Yung (Long Time); Joyce Mackenzie (Ruby); Marion Marshall (Annie); Marilyn Monroe (Clara); Barbara Smith (Julie).

Song: "Oh, What a Forward Young Man You Are"

Release date: May 19, 1950, Run time: 90 minutes.

The Asphalt Jungle

A Metro-Goldwyn-Mayer Picture (1950)

Arthur Hornblow Jr. (Producer); John Huston (Director); Ben Maddow and John Huston (Screenplay) from novel by W. R. Burnett; Harold Rosson (Photography); Miklós Rózsa (Music); Eugene Zador (Orchestration); Cedric Gibbons and Randall Duell (Art Directors); Edwin B. Willis (Set Decoration), Jack D. Moore (Associate); Jack Dawn (Makeup); Sydney Guilaroff (Hairstylist); Douglas Shearer and Robert B. Lee (Sound); Jack Greenwood (Assistant Director); George Boemler (Editor).

Cast: Sterling Hayden (Dix Handley); Louis Calhern (Alonzo D. Emmerich); Jean Hagen (Doll Conovan); James Whitmore (Gus Minissi); Sam Jaffe (Doc Erwin Riedenschneider); John McIntire (Police Commissioner Hardy); Marc Lawrence ("Cobby" Cobb); Barry Kelley (Detective Lieutenant Ditrich); Anthony Caruso (Louis Ciavelli); Teresa Celli (Maria Ciavelli); Marilyn Monroe (Angela Phinlay).

Release date: May 23, 1950, Run time: 112 minutes.

The Fireball

A Thor Production, released by 20th Century-Fox (1950)

Bert Friedlob (Producer); Tay Garnett (Director); Horace McCoy (Screenplay) from story by Tay Garnett and Horace McCoy; Lester White (Photography); Victor Young (Music); Leo Shuken and Sid Cuttner (Orchestration); Van Nest Polglase (Art Director); Richard Staub (Wardrobe); Agnes Flanagan (Hairstylist); Edward Voight (Makeup); William Fox (Sound); Charles Kerr (Assistant Director); Frank Sullivan (Editor).

Cast: Mickey Rooney (Johnny Casar); Pat O'Brien (Father O'Hara); Beverly Tyler (Mary Reeves); Glenn Corbett (Mack Miller); James Brown (Allen); Ralph Dumke (Bruno Crystal); Milburn Stone (Jeff Davis); Bert Begley (Shilling); Marilyn Monroe (Polly); Sam Flint (Dr. Barton); John Hedloe (Ullman).

Release Date: November 9, 1950, Run time: 84 minutes.

Right Cross

A Metro-Goldwyn-Mayer Picture (1950)

Armand Deutsch (Producer); John Sturges (Director); Charles Schnee (Screenplay); Norbert Brodine (Photography); David Raksin (Musical Director); Cedric Gibbons and Gabriel Scognamillo (Art Director); Edwin B. Willis (Set Decoration), Alfred E. Spencer (Associate); Helen Rose (Women's Costumes); Sydney Guilaroff (Hairstylist); Jack Dawn (Makeup); Douglas Shearer and Robert B. Lee (Sound); Dolph Zimmer (Assistant Director); James E. Newcom (Editor); John Indrisano (Technical Advisor).

Cast: June Allyson (Pat O'Malley); Dick Powell (Rick Garvey); Ricardo Montalban (Johnny Monterez); Lionel Barrymore (Sean O'Malley); Teresa Celli (Marina Monterez); Barry Kelley (Allan Goff); Tom Powers (Tom Balford); Mimi Aguglia (Mom Monterez); Marianne Stewart (Audrey); John Gallaudet (Phil Tripp); Wally Maher (First Reporter); Larry Keating (Second Reporter); Kenneth Tobey (Third Reporter); Bert Davidson (Fourth Reporter); Marilyn Monroe (Dusky Ledoux).

Release date: November 15, 1950, Run time: 90 minutes.

All About Eve

A 20th Century-Fox Picture (1950)

Darryl F. Zanuck (Producer); Joseph L. Mankiewicz (Director and Screenplay) from story by Mary Orr, Erich Käster (German version); Milton Krasner (Photography); Fred Sersen (Photographic Effects); Alfred Newman (Music); Edward Powell (Orchestration); Lyle Wheeler and George W. Davis (Art Directors); Thomas Little and Walter M. Scott (Set Decoration); Charles Le Maire (Wardrobe Director); Edith Head (Bette Davis's Costumes); Ben Nye (Makeup); W. D. Flick, Roger Heman, and Thomas T. Moulton (Sound); Barbara McLean (Editor).

Release date: October 14, 1950, Run time: 138 minutes.

Cast: Bette Davis (Margo Channing); Anne Baxter (Eve Harrington); George Sanders (Addison DeWitt); Celeste Holm (Karen Richards); Gary Merrill (Bill Sampson); Hugh Marlowe (Lloyd Richards); Gregory Ratoff (Max Fabian); Thelma Ritter (Birdie Coonan); Marilyn Monroe (Claudia Caswell); Barbara Bates (Phoebe); Walter Hampden (Aged Actor); Randy Stuart (Girl); Craig Hill (Leading Man); Leland Harris (Doorman); Barbara White (Autograph Seeker); Ed Fisher (Stage Manager); William Pullen (Clerk); Claude Stroud (Pianist); Eugene Borden (Frenchman); Helen Mowery (Reporter); Steven Geray (Captain of Waiters); Bess Flowers (Well-Wisher).

Song: "Liebestraum" (Franz Liszt).

Hometown Story

A Metro-Goldwyn-Mayer Picture (1951)

Arthur Pierson (Producer, Director, and Screenplay); Lucien Andriot (Photography); Louis Forbes (Music); Hilyard Brown (Art Director); Claude Carpenter (Set Decoration); Robert Littlefield (Makeup); William Randall (Sound); Richard Dixon (Assistant Director); William Claxton (Editor).

Release date: May 1951, Run time: 61 minutes.

Cast: Jeffrey Lynn (Blake Washburn); Donald Crisp (John MacFarland); Marjorie Reynolds (Janice Hunt); Alan Hale, Jr. (Slim Haskins); Marilyn Monroe (Iris Martin); Melinda Plowman (Katie Washburn); Barbara Brown (Mrs. Washburn); Virginia Campbell (Phoebe Hartman); Rennie McEvoy (Leo, the Taxi Driver); Glenn Tryon (Ken Kenlock); Byron Foulger (Berny Miles); Griff Barnett (Uncle Cliff Washburn); Harry Harvey (Andy Butterworth); Nelson Leigh (Dr. Johnson); Speck Noblitt (Motorcycle Officer).

As Young as You Feel

A 20th Century-Fox Picture (1951)

Lamar Trotti (Producer); Harmon Jones (Director); Lamar Trotti (Screenplay) from story by Paddy Chayefsky; Joseph MacDonald (Photography); Fred Sersen (Photographic Effects); Cyril Mockridge (Music); Lionel Newman (Musical Director); Maurice dePackh (Orchestration); Lyle Wheeler and Maurice Ransford (Art Directors); Thomas Little and Bruce MacDonald (Set Decoration); Charles Le Maire (Wardrobe Director); Renié (Costumes); Ben Nye (Makeup); W. D. Flick and Roger Heman (Sound); Robert Simpson (Editor).

Release date: August 2, 1951, Run time: 77 minutes.

Cast: Monty Woolley (John R. Hodges); Thelma Ritter (Della Hodges); David Wayne (Joe Elliot); Jean Peters (Alice Hodges); Constance Bennett (Lucille McKinley); Marilyn Monroe (Harriet); Allyn Joslyn (George Hodges); Albert Dekker (Louis McKinley); Clinton Sundberg (Frank Erickson); Minor Watson (Harold P. Cleveland); Wally Brown (Horace Gallagher); Russ Tamblyn (Willie McKinley); Don Beddoe (Head of Sales); Harry Shannon (Detective Kleinbaum); Renie Riano (Harpist).

Songs: "You Make Me Feel So Young" (Josef Myrow and Mack Gordon), "Born To Be Kissed" (Arthur Schwartz and Howard Dietz), "Consolidated March" (Alfred Newman and Cyril Mockridge), "Mama Inez" (E. Grenet and L. W. Gilbert).

Love Nest

A 20th Century-Fox Picture (1951)

Jules Buck (Producer); Joseph Newman (Director); I. A. L. Diamond (Screenplay) from novel by Scott Corbett; Lloyd Ahern (Photography); Fred Sersen (Photographic Effects); Cyril Mockridge (Music); Lionel Newman (Musical Director); Bernard Mayers (Orchestration); Lyle Wheeler and George L. Patrick (Art Directors); Thomas Little and Bruce Macdonald (Set Decoration); Charles Le Maire (Wardrobe Director); Renié (Costumes); Ben Nye (Makeup); Bernard Freericks and Harry M. Leonard (Sound); J. Watson Webb, Jr. (Editor).

Release date: October 10, 1951, Run time: 84 minutes.

Cast: June Haver (Connie Scott); William Lundigan (Jim Scott); Frank Fay (Charley Patterson); Marilyn Monroe (Roberta Stevens); Jack Paar (Ed Forbes); Leatrice Joy (Eadie Gaynor); Henry Kulky (George Hodges); Marie Blake (Mrs. Quigg); Patricia Miller (Florence); Maude Wallace (Mrs. Arnold); Joe Ploski (Mr. Hansen); Martha Wentworth (Mrs. Thompson); Faire Binney (Mrs. Frazier); Caryl Lincoln (Mrs. McNab); Michael Ross (Mr. McNab); Bob Jellison (Mr. Fain); John Costello (Postman); Charles Calvert (Mr. Knowland); Leo Cleary (Detective Donovan); Jack Daly (Mr. Clark); Ray Montgomery (Mr. Gray); Florence Auer (Mrs. Braddock); Edna Holland (Mrs. Engstrand); Liz Slifer (Mrs. Healy); Alvin Hammer (Glazier).

Let's Make it Legal

A 20th Century-Fox Picture (1951)

Robert Bassler (Producer); Richard Sale (Director); F. Hugh Herbert and I. A. L. Diamond (Screenplay) from story by Mortimer Braus; Lucien Ballard (Photography); Fred Sersen (Photographic Effects); Cyril Mockridge (Music); Lionel Newman (Musical Director); Edward Powell and Bernard Mayers (Orchestration); Lyle Wheeler and Albert Hogsett (Art Directors); Thomas Little and Paul S. Fox (Set Decoration); Charles Le Maire (Wardrobe Director); Renié (Costumes); Ben Nye (Makeup); E. Clayton Ward and Harry M. Leonard (Sound); Eli Dunn (Assistant Director); Robert Fritch (Editor).

Release date: November 6, 1951, Run time: 77 minutes.

Cast: Claudette Colbert (Miriam Halsworth); Macdonald Carey (Hugh Halsworth); Zachary Scott (Victor Macfarland); Barbara Bates (Barbara Denham); Robert Wagner (Jerry Denham); Marilyn Monroe (Joyce Mannering); Frank Cady (Ferguson); Jim Hayward (Pete, the Gardener); Carol Savage (Miss Jessup); Paul Gerrits (Milkman); Betty Jane Bowen (Secretary); Vicki Raaf (Peggy, Hugh's Secretary); Ralph Sanford (Police Lieutenant); Harry Denny (Hotel Manager); Harry Harvey, Sr. (Postman); Abe Dinovitch (Laborer); Joan Fisher (Baby Annabella); Kathleen Freeman (Reporter); James Magill (Reporter); Jack Mather (Policeman); Rennie McEvoy (Reporter); Roger Moore (Reporter); Michael Ross (Policeman); Frank Sully (Laborer); Beverly Thompson (Reporter); Wilson Wood (Reporter).

Clash by Night

A Jerry Wald-Norman Krasna Production, released by RKO (1952)

Harriet Parsons (Producer); Fritz Lang (Director); Alfred Hayes (Screenplay) from play by Clifford Odets; Nicholas Musuraca (Photography); Harold Wellman (Special Effects); Roy Webb (Music); C. Bakaleinikoff (Musical Director); Albert S. D'Agostino and Carroll Clark (Art Directors); Darrell Silvera and Jack Mills (Set Decoration); Michael Woulfe (Wardrobe Director); Mel Berns (Makeup); Larry Germain (Hairstylist); Jean L. Speak and Clem Portman (Sound); George Amy (Editor).

Release date: June 18, 1952, Run time: 105 minutes.

Cast: Barbara Stanwyck (Mae Doyle D'Amato); Paul Douglas (Jerry D'Amato); Robert Ryan (Earl Pfeiffer); Marilyn Monroe (Peggy); J. Carrol Naish (Uncle Vince); Keith Andes (Joe Doyle); Silvio Minciotti (Papa D'Amato).

Song: "I Hear a Rhapsody" (Jack Baker and Joe Gasparre).

We're Not Married

A 20th Century-Fox Picture (1952)

Nunnally Johnson (Producer and Screenplay); Edmund Goulding (Director); Gina Kaus and Jay Dratler (Story), Dwight Taylor (Adaptation); Leo Tover (Photography); Ray Kellogg (Photographic Effects); Cyril Mockridge (Music); Lionel Newman (Musical Director); Bernard Mayers (Orchestration); Lyle Wheeler and Leland Fuller (Art Directors); Thomas Little and Claude E. Carpenter (Set Decoration); Charles Le Maire (Wardrobe Director); Eloise Jensson (Costumes); Ben Nye (Makeup); Helen Turpin (Hairstylist); W. D Flick and Roger Heman (Sound); Paul Helmick (Assistant Director); Louis Loeffler (Editor).

Release date: July 11, 1952, Run time: 86 minutes.

Cast: Ginger Rogers (Ramona Gladwyn); Fred Allen (Steve Gladwyn); Victor Moore (Justice of the Peace Melvin Bush); Marilyn Monroe (Annabel Jones Norris); David Wayne (Jeff Norris); Eve Arden (Katie Woodruff); Paul Douglas (Hector Woodruff); Eddie Bracken (Willie Fisher); Mitzi Gaynor (Patsy Reynolds Fisher); Louis Calhern (Freddie Melrose); Zsa Zsa Gabor (Eve Melrose); James Gleason (Duffy); Paul Stewart (Attorney Stone); Jane Darwell (Mrs. Bush).

Don't Bother to Knock

A 20th Century-Fox Picture (1952)

Julian Blaustein (Producer); Roy Baker (Director); Daniel Taradash (Screenplay) from novel by Charlotte Armstrong; Lucien Ballard (Photography); Ray Kellogg (Photographic Effects); Lionel Newman (Musical Director); Earle Hagen and Bernard Mayers (Orchestration); Lyle Wheeler and Richard Irvine (Art Directors); Thomas Little and Paul S. Fox (Set Decoration); Charles Le Maire (Wardrobe Director); Travilla (Costumes); Ben Nye (Makeup); Bernard Freericks and Harry M. Leonard (Sound); George A. Gittens (Editor).

Release date: July 18, 1952, Run time: 76 minutes.

Cast: Richard Widmark (Jed Towers); Marilyn Monroe (Nell Forbes); Anne Bancroft (Lyn Lesley); Donna Corcoran (Bunny Jones); Jeanne Cagney (Rochelle); Lurene Tuttle (Ruth Jones); Elisha Cook, Jr. (Eddie Forbes); Jim Backus (Peter Jones); Verna Felton (Mrs. Emma Ballew); Willis Bouchey (Joe, the Bartender); Don Beddoe (Mr. Ballew); Gloria Blondell (Janey); Grace Hayle (Mrs. McMurdock); Michael Ross (Pat, the House Detective).

Songs: "Panic in the Streets" (Alfred Newman); "How About You" (Burton Lane and Ralph Freed); "A Rollin' Stone" (Lionel Newman, Ken Darby, and Bob Russell); "(I'll Take) Manhattan" (Richard Rodgers and Lorenz Hart); "There's a Lull in My Life," "Chattanooga Choo Choo" (Harry Warren and Mack Gordon); "How Blue the Night" (Jimmy McHugh and Harold Adamson).

Monkey Business

A 20th Century-Fox Picture (1952)

Sol C. Siegel (Producer); Howard Hawks (Director); Ben Hecht, Charles Lederer, and I. A. L. Diamond (Screenplay) from story by Harry Segall; Milton Krasner (Photography); Ray Kellogg (Photographic Effects); Leigh Harline (Music); Lionel Newman (Musical Director); Earle Hagen (Orchestration); Lyle Wheeler and George Patrick (Art Directors); Thomas Little and Walter M. Scott (Set Decoration); Charles Le Maire (Wardrobe Director); Travilla (Costumes); Ben Nye (Makeup); Helen Turpin (Hairstylist); W. D. Flick and Roger Heman (Sound); Paul Helmick and Don Torpin (Assistant Directors); William B. Murphy (Editor).

Release date: September 5, 1952, Run time: 97 minutes.

Cast: Cary Grant (Barnaby Fulton); Ginger Rogers (Edwina Fulton); Charles Coburn (Oliver Oxly); Marilyn Monroe (Lois Laurel); Hugh Marlowe (Hank Entwhistle); Henri Letondal (Dr. Jerome Lenton); Robert Cornthwaite (Dr. Zoldeck); Larry Keating (G. J. Culverly); Douglas Spencer (Dr. Brunner); Esther Dale (Mrs. Rhinelander); George Winslow (Little Indian).

Song: "The Whiffenpoof Song" (Tod B. Galloway, Meade Minnigerode, and George S. Pomeroy).

O. Henry's Full House

A 20th Century-Fox Picture (1952)

Andre Hakim (Producer); Directors: Henry Koster ("The Cop and the Anthem"), Henry Hathaway ("The Clarion Call"), Jean Negulesco ("The Last Leaf"), Howard Hawks ("The Ransom of Red Chief"), Henry King ("The Gift of the Magi"); Screenplays: Lamar Trotti ("The Cop and the Anthem"), Richard L. Breen ("The Clarion Call"), Ivan Goff and Ben Roberts ("The Last Leaf"), Nunnally Johnson, Charles Lederer, and Ben Hecht ("Ransom of Red Chief"), Walter Bullock ("The Gift of the Magi") from stories by O. Henry; Lloyd Ahern, Lucien Ballard, Milton R. Krasner, and Joseph MacDonald (Photography); Alfred Newman (Music); Edward B. Powell (Orchestration); Lyle Wheeler, Joseph C. Wright, Chester Gore, Addison Hehr, and Richard Irvine (Art Directors); Thomas Little, Fred J. Rode, Claude E. Carpenter, and Bruce MacDonald (Set Decoration); Charles Le Maire (Wardrobe Director); Edward Stevenson (Costumes); Barbara McLean, Nick DeMaggio, and William B. Murphy (Editors).

Release date: October 16, 1952, Run time: 118 minutes.

Cast: John Steinbeck (Narrator); "The Cop and the Anthem": Charles Laughton (Soapy), Marilyn Monroe (Streetwalker), David Wayne (Horace); "The Clarion Call": Richard Widmark (Johnny Kernan), Dale Robertson (Barney Woods), Richard Rober (Chief of Detectives); "The Last Leaf": Anne Baxter (Joanna Goodwin), Jean Peters (Susan Goodwin), Gregory Ratoff (Behrman), Richard Garrick (Doctor); "The Ransom of Red Chief": Fred Allen (Sam Slick Brown), Oscar Levant (Bill Peoria), Lee Aaker (J. B. Dorset); "The Gift of the Magi": Jeanne Crain (Della), Farley Granger (Jim), Fred Kelsey (Santa Claus).

Niagara

A 20th Century-Fox Picture (1953)

Charles Brackett (Producer); Henry Hathaway (Director); Charles Brackett, Walter Reisch, and Richard Breen (Screenplay); Joseph MacDonald (Photography); Leonard Doss (Technicolor Color Consultant); Ray Kellogg (Photographic Effects); Sol Kaplan (Music); Lionel Newman (Musical Director); Edward Powell (Orchestration); Lyle Wheeler and Maurice Ransford (Art Directors); Stuart Reiss (Set Decoration); Charles Le Maire (Wardrobe Director); Dorothy Jeakins (Costumes); Ben Nye (Makeup); W. D. Flick and Roger Heman (Sound); Gerd Oswald (Assistant Director); Barbara McLean (Editor).

Release date: January 21, 1953, Run time: 89 minutes.

Cast: Marilyn Monroe (Rose Loomis); Joseph Cotten (George Loomis); Jean Peters (Polly Cutler); Casey Adams (Ray Cutler); Denis O'Dea (Inspector Starkey); Richard Allan (Ted Patrick); Don Wilson (Mr. Kettering); Lurene Tuttle (Mrs. Kettering); Russell Collins (Mr. Qua); Will Wright (Boatman); Lester Matthews (Doctor); Carleton Young (Policeman).

Song: "Kiss" (Lionel Newman and Haven Gillespie).

Gentlemen Prefer Blondes

A 20th Century-Fox Picture (1953)

Sol C. Siegel (Producer); Howard Hawks (Director); Charles Lederer (Screenplay) from musical play by Anita Loos and Joseph Fields and novel by Anita Loos; Harry J. Wild (Photography); Leonard Doss (Technicolor Color Consultant); Ray Kellogg (Photographic Effects); Lionel Newman (Musical Director); Herbert Spencer, Earle Hagen, and Bernard Mayers (Orchestration); Eliot Daniel (Vocal Director); Jack Cole (Choreographer); Lyle Wheeler and Joseph C. Wright (Art Directors); Claude E. Carpenter (Set Decoration); Charles Le Maire (Wardrobe Director); Travilla (Costumes); Ben Nye (Makeup); E. Clayton Ward and Roger Heman (Sound); Paul Helmick (Assistant Director); Hugh S. Fowler (Editor).

Release date: July 15, 1953, Run time: 91 minutes.

Cast: Jane Russell (Dorothy Shaw); Marilyn Monroe (Lorelei Lee); Charles Coburn (Sir Francis "Piggy" Beekman); Elliott Reid (Detective Ernie Malone); Tommy Noonan (Gus Esmond); George Winslow (Henry Spofford III); Marcel Dalio (Magistrate); Taylor Holmes (Mr. Esmond, Sr.); Norma Varden (Lady Beekman); Howard Wendell (Watson); Steven Geray (Hotel Manager); Henri Letondal (Grotier, the Prosecutor); Leo Mostovoy (Phillipe); Alex Frazer (Pritchard); George Davis (Pierre, the Cab Driver); Alphonse Martell (Headwaiter at Chez Louis); Jimmie Moultrie (Dancer); Freddie Moultrie (Dancer); George Chakiris (Dancer).

Songs: "Two Little Girls from Little Rock," "Bye Bye Baby," "Diamonds Are a Girl's Best Friend" (Jule Styne and Leo Robin); "Anyone Here for Love," "When Love Goes Wrong" (Hoagy Carmichael and Harold Adamson).

How to Marry a Millionaire

A 20th Century-Fox Picture (1953)

Nunnally Johnson (Producer and Screenplay); Jean Negulesco (Director); Nunnally Johnson (Screenplay) from plays by Zoe Akins and Dale Eunson and Katherine Albert; Joseph MacDonald (Photography); Leonard Doss (Technicolor Color Consultant); Ray Kellogg (Special Effects); Cyril Mockridge (Incidental Music); Alfred Newman (Musical Director); Edward B. Powell (Orchestration); Lyle Wheeler and Leland Fuller (Art Directors); Walter M. Scott and Stuart Reiss (Set Decoration); Charles Le Maire (Wardrobe Director); Travilla (Costumes); Ben Nye (Makeup); Alfred Bruzlin and Roger Heman (Sound); F. E. Johnston (Assistant Director); Louis Loeffler (Editor).

Release date: November 5, 1953, Run time: 95 minutes.

Cast: Betty Grable (Loco Dempsey); Marilyn Monroe (Pola Debevoise); Lauren Bacall (Schatze Page); David Wayne (Freddie Denmark); Rory Calhoun (Eben); Cameron Mitchell (Tom Brookman); Alex D'Arcy (J. Stewart Merrill); Fred Clark (Waldo Brewster); William Powell (J. D. Hanley); George Dunn (Mike, the Elevator Operator); Percy Helton (Mr. Benton); Robert Adler (Cab Driver); Tudor Owen (Furniture Buyer); Maurice Marsac (Mr. Antione); Hermine Sterler (Madame); Abney Mott (Tom's Secretary); Charlotte Austin (Ding-Dong); Merry Anders, Ruth Hall, Beryl McCutcheon, Lida Thomas (Fashion Models).

Songs: "Street Scene" (Alfred Newman); "New York" (Lionel Newman and Ken Darby).

River of No Return

A 20th Century-Fox Picture (1954)

Stanley Rubin (Producer); Otto Preminger (Director); Frank Fenton (Screenplay) from story by Louis Lantz; Joseph LaShelle (Photography), Leonard Doss (Technicolor Color Consultant); Ray Kellogg (Photographic Effects); Cyril J. Mockridge (Music); Lionel Newman (Musical Director); Edward B. Powell (Orchestration); Ken Darby (Vocal Director); Jack Cole (Choreography); Lyle Wheeler and Addison Hehr (Art Directors); Walter M. Scott and Chester Bayhi (Set Decoration); Charles Le Maire (Wardrobe Director); Travilla (Costumes); Ben Nye (Makeup); Bernard Freericks and Roger Heman (Sound); Paul Helmick and Donald C. Klune (Assistant Directors); Louis Loeffler (Editor).

Release date: April 30, 1954, Run time: 91 minutes.

Cast: Robert Mitchum (Matt Calder); Marilyn Monroe (Kay Weston); Rory Calhoun (Harry Weston); Tommy Rettig (Mark Calder); Murvyn Vye (Dave Colby); Douglas Spencer (Sam Benson); Ed Hinton (Gambler); Don Beddoe (Ben).

Songs: "I'm Gonna File My Claim," "One Silver Dollar," "Down in the Meadow," "River of No Return" (Lionel Newman and Ken Darby).

There's No Business Like Show Business

A 20th Century-Fox Picture (1954)

Sol C. Siegel (Producer); Walter Lang (Director); Phoebe and Henry Ephron (Screenplay) from story by Lamar Trotti (Story); Leon Shamroy (Photography); Leonard Doss (DeLuxe Color Consultant); Ray Kellogg (Photographic Effects); Alfred Newman and Lionel Newman (Musical Directors); Edward B. Powell, Earle Hagen, Herbert Spencer, and Bernard Mayers (Orchestration); Ken Darby (Vocal Director); Hal Schaefer (Vocal Arrangements); Robert Alton and Jack Cole (Choreographers); Lyle Wheeler and John DeCuir (Art Directors); Walter M. Scott and Stuart Reiss (Set Decoration); Charles Le Maire (Wardrobe Director); Miles White and Travilla (Costumes); Ben Nye (Makeup); Helen Turpin (Hairstylist); E. Clayton Ward and Murray Spivack (Sound); Ad Schaumer (Assistant Director); Robert Simpson (Editor).

Release date: December 16, 1954, Run Time: 117 minutes.

Cast: Ethel Merman (Molly Donahue); Donald O'Connor (Tim Donahue); Marilyn Monroe (Vicky); Dan Dailey (Terry Donahue); Johnnie Ray (Steve Donahue); Mitzi Gaynor (Katy Donahue); Richard Eastham (Lew Harris); Hugh O'Brian (Charles Biggs); Frank McHugh (Eddie Dugan); Rhys Williams (Father Dineen); Lee Patrick (Marge); Eve Miller (Hat-check Girl); Robin Raymond (Lillian Sawyer); Lyle Talbot (Stage Manager); Alvy Moore (Katy's Boyfriend); Chick Chandler (Harry); Nolan Leary (Archbishop); Henry Slate (Dance Director); Gavin Gordon (Geoffrey Miles).

Songs: "When the Midnight Choo-Choo Leaves for Alabam'," "Play a Simple Melody," "A Pretty Girl is Like a Melody," "You'd Be Surprised," "Alexander's Ragtime Band," "After You Get What You Want You Don't Want It," "Remember," "If You Believe," "A Man Chases a Girl (Until She Catches Him)," "Heat Wave," "Lazy," "A Sailor's Not a Sailor ('Til a Sailor's Been Tattooed)," "Let's Have Another Cup of Coffee," "There's No Business Like Show Business" (Irving Berlin).

The Seven Year Itch

A 20th Century-Fox Production (1955)

Charles K. Feldman and Billy Wilder (Producers), Doane Harrison (Associate); Billy Wilder (Director); Billy Wilder and George Axelrod (Screenplay) from play by George Axelrod; Milton Krasner (Photography); Ray Kellogg (Photographic Effects); Leonard Doss (DeLuxe Color Consultant); Alfred Newman (Musical Director); Edward B. Powell (Orchestration); Lyle Wheeler and George W. Davis (Art Directors); Walter M. Scott and Stuart A. Reiss (Set Decoration); Charles Le Maire (Wardrobe Director); Travilla (Costumes); Ben Nye (Makeup); Helen Turpin (Hairstylist); E. Clayton Ward and Harry M. Leonard (Sound); Joseph E. Rickards (Assistant Director); Hugh S. Fowler (Editor).

Release date: June 3, 1955, Run time: 105 minutes.

Cast: Marilyn Monroe (The Girl); Tom Ewell (Richard Sherman); Evelyn Keyes (Helen Sherman); Sonny Tufts (Tom MacKenzie); Robert Strauss (Mr. Kruhulik); Oskar Homolka (Dr. Brubaker); Marguerite Chapman (Miss Morris); Victor Moore (Plumber); Roxanne (Elaine); Donald MacBride (Mr. Brady); Carolyn Jones (Miss Finch); Butch Bernard (Ricky Sherman); Doro Merande (Waitress); Dorothy Ford (Indian Girl).

Song: "Second piano concerto" (Sergei Rachmaninov).

Bus Stop

A 20th Century-Fox Picture (1956)

Buddy Adler (Producer); Joshua Logan (Director); George Axelrod (Screenplay) from play by William Inge; Milton R. Krasner (Photography); Leonard Doss (Technicolor Color Consultant); Ray Kellogg (Photographic Effects); Alfred Newman and Cyril J. Mockridge (Music); Edward B. Powell (Orchestration); Ken Darby (Vocal Director); Lyle R. Wheeler and Mark-Lee Kirk (Art Directors); Walter M. Scott and Paul S. Fox (Set Decoration); Charles Le Maire (Wardrobe Designer); Travilla (Costumes); Ben Nye (Makeup); Helen Turpin (Hairstylist); Alfred Bruzlin and Harry M. Leonard (Sound); Ben Kadish (Assistant Director); William Reynolds (Editor).

Release date: August 31, 1956, Run time: 96 minutes.

Cast: Marilyn Monroe (Cherie); Don Murray (Beauregard "Bo" Decker); Arthur O'Connell (Virgil Blessing); Betty Field (Grace); Eileen Heckart (Vera); Robert Bray (Carl); Hope Lange (Elma Duckworth); Hans Conreid (Life Magazine Photographer); Casey Adams (Life Magazine Reporter); Henry Slate (Manager of Blue Dragon); Terry Kelman (Gerald); Linda Brace (Evelyn).

Songs: "The Bus Stop Song" (Ken Darby); "That Old Black Magic" (Harold Arlen and Johnny Mercer).

The Prince and the Showgirl

A Marilyn Monroe Production, released by Warner Bros. (1957)

Laurence Olivier (Producer and Director); Hugh Perceval (Production Executive); Milton Anthony Bushell (Associate Director); Terrence Rattigan (Screenplay) from play *The Sleeping Prince* by Terrence Rattigan; Jack Cardiff (Photography); Bill Warrington and Charles Staffell (Special Effects); Richard Addinsell (Music); Muir Mathieson (Musical Director); Roger Furse (Production Designer); Carmen Dillon (Art Director); Dario Simoni (Set Decoration); Beatrice Dawson (Costumes); Toni Sforzini (Makeup); Gordon Bond (Hairstylist); John Mitchell and Gordon McCallum (Sound); David Orton (Assistant Director); Jack Harris (Editor); Elaine Schreyek (Continuity).

Release date: June 13, 1957, Run Time: 117 minutes.

Cast: Marilyn Monroe (Elsie Marina); Laurence Olivier (Grand Duke Charles); Sybil Thorndike (Queen Dowager); Jeremy Spencer (King Nicolas); Richard Wattis (Northbrook); Jean Ken (Maisie Springfield); Esmond Knight (Colonel Hoffman); Paul Hardwick (Major Domo); Rosamund Greenwood (Maud); Aubrey Dexter (Ambassador); Maxine Audley (Lady Sunningdale); Andreas Malandrinos (Valet with Violin); Daphne Anderson (Fanny); Gillian Owen (Maggie); Vera Day (Betty).

Song: "I Found a Dream"

Some Like it Hot

A Metro-Goldwyn-Mayer Picture (1959)

Billy Wilder (Producer and Director); Doane Harrison and I. A. L. Diamond (Associate Producers); Billy Wilder and I. A. L. Diamond (Screenplay) from story by Robert Thoeren and Michael Logan; Charles Lang, Jr. (Photography); Milt Rice (Special Effects); Adolph Deutsch (Music); Eve Newman (Music Editor); Matty Malneck (Song Supervisor); Ted Haworth (Art Director); Edward G. Boyle (Set Decoration); Orry-Kelly (Costumes); Emile LaVigne (Makeup); Alice Monte and Agnes Flanagan (Hairstylists); Fred Lau (Sound); Sam Nelson (Assistant Director); Arthur P. Schmidt (Editor); Allen K. Wood (Production Manager); Tom Plews (Props); John Franco (Continuity).

Release date: March 29, 1959, Run time: 122 minutes.

Cast: Marilyn Monroe (Sugar "Kane" Kowalczyk); Tony Curtis (Joe—"Josephine"); Jack Lemmon (Jerry—"Daphne"); George Raft (Spats Columbo); Pat O'Brien (Mulligan); Joe E. Brown (Osgood Fielding III); Nehemiah Persoff (Little Bonaparte); Joan Shawlee (Sweet Sue); Billy Gray (Sig Poliakoff); George E. Stone (Toothpick Charlie); Dave Barry (Beinstock); Mike Mazurki (Henchman); Harry Wilson (Henchman); Beverly Wills (Dolores); Barbara Drew (Nellie); Edward G. Robinson, Jr. (Johnny Paradise); Marian Collier (Olga); Helen Perry (Rosella); Al Breneman (Bellhop); Laurie Mitchell (Mary Lou); Tito Vuolo (Mozzarella).

Songs: "Runnin' Wild," "Down Among the Sheltering Palms" (A. H. Gibbs, Joe Grey, and Leo Wood); "By the Beautiful Sea" (Harry Carroll and Harold Atteridge); "I Wanna Be Loved by You" (Bert Kalmar, Herbert Wood, and Harry Ruby); "I'm Through with Love" (Gus Kahn, Matty Malneck, and Jay Livingston).

Let's Make Love

A 20th Century-Fox Picture (1960)

Jerry Wald (Producer); George Cukor (Director); Norman Krasna (Screenplay), Hal Kanter and Arthur Miller (Additional Material); Daniel L. Fapp (Photography); Lionel Newman (Musical Director), Earle H. Hagen (Associate); Jack Cole (Choreographer); Lyle Wheeler and Gene Allen (Art Directors); Walter M. Scott and Fred M. MacLean (Set Decoration); Dorothy Jeakins (Costumes); Ben Nye (Makeup); Helen Turpin (Hairstylist); W. D. Flick and Warren B. Delaplain (Sound); David Hall (Assistant Director); David Bretherton (Editor).

Release date: September 8, 1960, Run time: 119 minutes.

Cast: Marilyn Monroe (Amanda Dell); Yves Montand (Jean-Marc Clement); Tony Randall (Alexander Coffman); Frankie Vaughan (Tony Danton); Wilfrid Hyde-White (John Wales); David Burns (Oliver Burton); Michael David (Dave Kerry); Mara Lynn (Lily Nyles); Dennis King, Jr. (Abe Miller); Joe Besser (Charlie Lamont); Harry Cheshire (Minister); Ray Foster (Jimmy); Milton Berle, Bing Crosby, and Gene Kelly (as themselves).

Songs: "Let's Make Love," "Hey You with the Crazy Eyes," "Sing Me a Song that Sells," "Specialization," "Incurably Romantic" (Jimmy Van Heusen and Sammy Cahn); "My Heart Belongs to Daddy" (Cole Porter).

The Misfits

A Seven Arts Production, released by United Artists (1961)

Frank E. Taylor (Producer); John Huston (Director); Arthur Miller (Screenplay); Russell Metty (Photography); Alex North (Music); Stephen Grimes and William Newberry (Art Directors); Frank McKelvy (Set Decoration); Jean Louis (Marilyn Monroe's Wardrobe); Allan Snyder, Frank Prehoda, and Frank La Rue (Makeup); Sydney Guilaroff and Agnes Flanagan (Hairstylists); Philip Mitchell and Charles Grenzbach (Sound); Edward Parone (Assistant to Producer); Carl Beringer (Assistant Director); Tom Shaw (Second Unit Director); Rex Wimpy (Second Unit Photography); George Tomasini (Editor); C. O. Erickson (Production Manager); Angela Allen (Script Supervisor); Billy Jones (Wrangler).

Release date: February 1, 1961, Run time: 124 minutes.

Cast: Clark Gable (Gay Langland); Marilyn Monroe (Roslyn Taber); Montgomery Clift (Perce Howland); Thelma Ritter (Isabelle Steers); Eli Wallach (Guido); James Barton (Old Man); Estelle Winwood (Church Lady); Kevin McCarthy (Raymond Taber); Dennis Shaw (Young Boy).

Something's Got to Give

A 20th Century-Fox Picture (1962)

Henry T. Weinstein (Producer), Gene Allen (Associate); George Cukor (Director); Nunnally Johnson and Walter Bernstein (Screenplay) from *My Favorite Wife* screenplay by Bella and Sam Spewack; William H. Daniels, Charles Lang, Franz Planer, and Leo Tover (Photography); Gene Allen (Art Director); Jean Louis (Costumes); Sydney Guilaroff (Hairstylist).

Cast: Marilyn Monroe (Ellen Wagstaff Arden); Dean Martin (Nicholas Arden); Cyd Charisse (Bianca Russell Arden); Tom Tryon (Stephen Burkett); Alexandra Heilweil (Lita Arden); Robert Christopher Morley (Timmy Arden); Wally Cox (Shoe Salesman); Phil Silvers (Insurance Salesman); John McGiver (Judge); Grady Sutton (Bailiff); Steve Allen (Psychiatrist).

Song: "Something's Got to Give" (Johnny Mercer).

910-X-143

THE SEVEN YEAR ITCH, 1955

Endnotes

Page 8: "I don't care": *Ms.*, August 1972, 41.

Page 10: For a time: *The American Film Institute Catalog, 1941-1950*, 2096.

Pages 14-15: "The Dangerous Years", Evie's exchanges: *Dangerous Years* file, Fox story file collection, Arts Library, UCLA (hereafter Fox-UCLA).

Page 16: The film also: *The American Film Institute Catalog, 1941-1950*, 2540.

Page 22: "I can see": *All About Eve* combined continuity script, Fox Story Department.

Page 23: "[Marilyn] seemed to": *All About Eve* Celeste Holm audio commentary, Twentieth Century-Fox Home Entertainment, 2003.

Pages 24, 25, 27, 28, 29: "You are in a beehive", "Fasten your seat belts", "Miss Caswell is an actress", "Tell me this. Do", "Oh waiter", "Why do they always", "Champion to champion", "Now there's something a girl": *All About Eve* combined continuity script, Fox Story Department.

Page 33: "This unpretentious little picture": *New York Times* film review, August 1951.

Pages 33-35: "Did you meet", "You know as", "Mr. McKinley control": *As Young as You Feel* script, Fox Story Department.

Page 37: The above, one: *Love Nest* file, Twentieth Century-Fox Collection, Special Collections, The Academy of Motion Picture Arts and Sciences (hereafter Fox-AMPAS).

Page 37: The author's original: *Love Nest* file, Fox-AMPAS.

Page 39: "Well, you wouldn't": *Love Nest* final shooting script, Fox Story Department.

Page 43: A Word from: *Love Nest* file, Production Code Administration papers, MPAA Collection, AMPAS (hereafter PCA-AMPAS).

Page 43: "You know, all", "Seems strange giving": *Love Nest* final shooting script, Fox Story Department.

Pages 48-49: "Honey, your father's", "Who wouldn't want", "My motor's been": *Let's Make it Legal* final shooting script, Fox Story Department.

Pages 52, 55: "You mean it means", Husband and Spectator: *We're Not Married* final shooting script, Fox Story Department.

Page 60: Casting Calls: *Don't Bother to Knock* file, Fox-AMPAS, Fox-UCLA.

Page 61: One Take Wonder: *Don't Bother to Knock* file, Fox-AMPAS, Fox-UCLA.

Pages 62-63, 65-67: "And please, don't", "Do you have", "I just wanted", "You came over", "I can't figure": *Don't Bother to Knock* final shooting script, Fox Story Department.

Page 68: A Word from: *Don't Bother to Knock* file, PCA-AMPAS.

Page 69: "Marilyn Monroe, co-starred": *Variety* film review, July 1952.

Pages 70, 72-78, 80: "Good morning", "Well, Miss Laurel", "You're old only", "Find someone to", Battling Blondes, On the Town, Skating Sensations, "Well, everybody looking", "Now say terrify": *Monkey Business* combined continuity script, October 1952, Fox Story Department.

Page 86: "Good afternoon my", "My compliments to": *O. Henry's Full House* continuity script, Fox Story Department.

Pages 89, 93-94, 97, 101-104, 106: "She's a tramp!", "Didn't that Mrs", "Hey, get out", "And parading around", "Sure I'm meeting", "There isn't any", The original plan, Other song swaps, "On the bed", After murdering Rose, "They can't play", "Why don't you", "You've been very": *Niagara* final shooting script, May 15, 1952, Fox Story Department.

Page 95: Casting Calls: *Niagara* file, Fox-AMPAS, Fox-UCLA.

Page 97: A Word from: *Niagara* file, PCA-AMPAS.

Page 97: "There should be": *Niagara* file, PCA-AMPAS.

Page 108: Further tipping the: *Gentlemen Prefer Blondes* file, Fox-AMPAS, Fox-UCLA.

Page 109: Marilyn's inability to: Russell, Jane, *Jane Russell: My Paths and My Detours* (New York: Franklin Watts, 1985), 138.

Page 113: Co-star Casting: *Gentlemen Prefer Blondes* file, Fox-AMPAS, Fox-UCLA.

Page 124: A Dream Come: Endres, Stacy and Robert Cushman, *Hollywood at Your Feet: The Story of the World Famous Chinese Theatre* (California: Pomegranate Press, 1997), 241, 242, 243.

Pages 126, 131-133, 136-137, 141, 145: "The way most", "You know what", "Men aren't attentive", "You don't think", "Pola writes with", Girl Talk, Double Frozen Daiquiris," "You know of", "What happened to": *How to Marry a Millionaire* revised final script, February 13, 1953, Fox Story Department.

Page 129: "The big question": Otis L. Guernsey, Jr., *New York Herald-Tribune*, 1953, 236.

Page 129: In a memo: Behlmer, Rudy, *Memo from Darryl F. Zanuck: The Golden Years at Twentieth Century-Fox* (New York: Grove Press, 1995).

Page 135: "She did an": McGee, Tom, *Betty Grable: The Girl with the Million Dollar Legs* (New York: Vestal, 1995), 260.

Page 136: Lauren Bacall, the: Bacall, Lauren, *By Myself* (New York: Knopf, 1979).

Page 139: Casting Calls, By the time: *How to Marry a Millionaire* file, Fox-AMPAS, Fox-UCLA.

Page 140: A Word from: *How to Marry a Millionaire* file, PCA-AMPAS.

Page 146: "The Indians call", "You get somebody", "Some other time", "This one and": *River of No Return* dialogue continuity, Fox Story Department.

Page 161: That spring Zanuck: Behlmer, Rudy, *Memo from Darryl F. Zanuck: The Golden Years at Twentieth Century-Fox* (New York: Grove Press, 1995).

Pages 163, 169: "That girl who", "Check your hat": *There's No Business Like Show Business* script, Fox Story Department.

Pages 172-174, 177-183, 187-188: "Hey! I just washed", "the sporadic infidelity", "When it's hot", "You may not", "I had onions", "I wouldn't be lying", On marriage, "A married man", "It shakes me", "Chopsticks! I can", "I think you're", "There I was", "Maybe if I", "Oh do you", "Ooh! Here comes", "This one's even": *The Seven Year Itch* script, Fox Story Department.

Page 172: Six words spoken: *Life,* September 27, 1954.

Page 191: "The thing I'd": *Person to Person*, CBS, April 1955.

Pages 194-197, 202-204, 207, 209: "For a weddin'", "You might say", California Dreaming, From the Cutting, A Girl's Best, Sections in blue, "Well, Cherry, you're", "I like ya", "I'd like for": *Bus Stop* final shooting script, February 27, 1956, Fox Story Department.

Page 198: Casting Calls: *Bus Stop* file, Fox-AMPAS, Fox-UCLA.

Page 201: A Word from: *Bus Stop* file, PCA-AMPAS.

Page 211: Looking for a Billionaire: *Let's Make Love* file, Fox-AMPAS, Fox-UCLA.

Pages 214, 216, 218, 223: "You can always tell", "There used to be", "The least you could", To Be Wonderful: *Let's Make Love* second revised shooting script, January 15, 1960, Fox Story Department.

Pages 226-228, 235, 241: That Certain Something, The Inspiration, In Production, Uncooperative Co-star, The Reconstruction: *Marilyn Monroe: The Final Days*, Twentieth Century-Fox Home Entertainment, 2001.

Pages 232, 234-235, 238, 240: "How long does it take", "Miss Ingrid Tic", "Honeymoon is over", "You know what", "Come on. The", "Will you have": *Something's Got to Give* script, Fox Story Department.

Select Bibliography

Production information gathered from original studio files and newspaper clipping collections at the Academy of Motion Picture Arts and Sciences, the UCLA Arts Library (Twentieth Century-Fox Collection), and the New York Public Library for the Performing Arts.

The American Film Institute Catalog of Motion Pictures Produced in the United States, 1941-1950. Berkeley: University of California Press, 1999.

Bacall, Lauren. *By Myself.* New York: Alfred A. Knopf, 1979.

Behlmer, Rudy. *Memo from Darryl F. Zanuck: The Golden Years at Twentieth Century-Fox.* New York: Grove Press, 1993.

Conway, Michael and Mark Ricci. *The Complete Films of Marilyn Monroe.* New York: Citadel Press, 1964, 1992.

Guiles, Fred Lawrence. *Legend: The Life and Death of Marilyn Monroe.* Lanham, MD: Scarborough House, 1984, 1992.

Haspiel, James. *Marilyn: The Ultimate Look at the Legend.* New York: Henry Holt and Company, 1991.

Haspiel, James. *Young Marilyn: Becoming the Legend.* New York: Hyperion, 1994.

Karney, Robyn. *Cinema Year by Year: 1894-2000.* London: Dorling Kindersley, 2001.

Monroe, Marilyn. *My Story.* New York: Stein & Day, 1974.

Spada, James with George Zeno. *Monroe: Her Life in Pictures.* New York: Doubleday, 1982.

Thomas, Tony and Aubrey Solomon. *The Films of Twentieth Century-Fox.* New York: Citadel Press, 1964, 1980.

Victor, Adam. *The Marilyn Encyclopedia.* Woodstock, NY: The Overlook Press, 1999.

NIAGARA, 1953

Acknowledgments

For making this book a reality, credit, as well as deep gratitude of the author, goes to many: 20th Century-Fox's extraordinary Debbie Olshan for making the project possible, to Nicole Spiegel, as well as the diligent staffs of the studio's Photo Archives and Story departments. Thank you to Running Press publisher Jon Anderson. Others indispensable in various ways during production of this book were Josh McDonnell, who applied his unique and beautiful vision to the design, Greg Jones, Rachel Cabrera, Daniel Siegel, Kelli Chipponeri, Jennifer Colella, Sarah O'Brien, and an invaluable research assistant and sister, Claudia De La Hoz. Also deserving of special mention are the staffs of the Academy of Motion Picture Arts and Sciences, the American Film Institute, the UCLA Arts Library, and the New York Public Library for the Performing Arts.

Index

260

Index